Unlocking Human Capital to Drive Performance

A CEO's Handbook

Unlocking Human Capital to Drive Performance

A CEO's Handbook

Sanjiv Anand
Managing Director
Cedar Management Consulting International, LLC
New York

Tata McGraw Hill Education Private Limited
NEW DELHI

McGraw-Hill Offices

New Delhi New York St Louis San Francisco Auckland Bogotá Caracas
Kuala Lumpur Libson London Madrid Mexico City Milan Montreal
San Juan Santiago Singapore Sydney Tokyo Toronto

Tata McGraw-Hill

Published by Tata McGraw Hill Education Private Limited,
7 West Patel Nagar, New Delhi 110008

First reprint 2012
RXLCRDDGRXLYZ

ISBN (13): 978-0-07-070714-6
ISBN (10): 0-07-070714-6

Vice President and Managing Director—Asia-Pacific Region: *Ajay Shukla*
Publishing Manager—Professional: *Vibhor Kataria*
Manager—Production: *Sohan Gaur*
AGM—Sales and Business Development: *S Girish*
Asst. Product Manager—Business and General Reference: *Priyanka Goel*
General Manager—Production: *Rajender P Ghansela*
Manager—Production: *Reji Kumar R.*

Typeset by SwaRadha Typesetting, 588 Pocket-5, Mayur Vihar-I, New Delhi 110091 and printed at Rajkamal Electric Press, Kundli 131 028, Haryana

Cover Printer: Rajkamal Electric Press
Cover Designer: Kapil Gupta
Illustrations by: Prriya Raj

The McGraw·Hill Companies

To

My father,
Dr. K.K. Anand,
the HR guru
who has taught me
everything in life!

The author thanks

Prriya Raj

for the illustrations in the book

Testimonials from Industry Leaders

"There is a lot of practical wisdom in Sanjiv's book from his long consulting experience. The book is easy to read and understand. It portrays a number of "real life" issues and lessons which can be implemented."

—Ajay Piramal, Chairman, Piramal Enteprises Ltd

"Sanjiv has captured the essence of Human Capital management superbly from the CEO's perspective in a very readable style."

—Rick Pudner, CEO, Emirates National Bank of Dubai (ENBD)

"Sanjiv has creatively captured the key challenges in HR that CEOs face. It is a must read for all senior managers who want to effectively deal with management talent from the top of the organization."

—Ron Sanders, President, Warner Home Video

"A very comprehensive book without any academic overload, vividly written, easy to read. It's right from the guts."

—Dr. Holger Hatty, Member of the Management Board, Swiss International Airlines

"Sanjiv manages to take both a bird's-eye view, as well as a worm's eye view of human resources at work. Human Capital has been clearly identified as a key differentiator between the high performance organizations and others. The book is clearly intended to help top management make insightful people-related decisions."

—Sunil Kant Munjal, JT Managing Director, Hero MotoCorp

"If you are in business for a long time you undoubtedly pick up a few management gems. Never in my reading have those gems been presented all together, so comprehensively and in plain English."

—Larry Borgard, President & CEO, Utilities, Integrys Energy Group, Inc.

"The book deals with very practical solutions with great insights from Sanjiv's personal experience. It would be a great handbook for the CEOs. I have no doubt that the readers would gain immensely, and at the same time enjoy the humor and simplicity of the style of writing."

—Akhil Gupta, Deputy Group CEO, Bharti Enterprises

"Wit and wisdom pepper Sanjiv's Strategic Imperatives. Research shows that successful CEOs spend almost 60% of their time on HR. By positioning HR firmly at the heart of strategy, Sanjiv reminds CEOs of the most important role they have to play, and offers practical solutions."

—Gita Piramal, Author, Business Maharajas and Managing Radical Change

"I truly believe that unlocking human capital will be the biggest competitive edge for any organisation in the next decade. Sanjiv has written on a very topical and relevant subject. It is full of pragmatic ideas presented in a simple, readable style that any CEO and HR practitioner will find useful."

—Leena Nair, Executive Director–HR, Hindustan Unilever Limited and VP–HR, South Asia

Preface

I am not a HR guru. Surely, I did study HR in my MBA program at NYU Stern, but as you all know, HR classes at a business school (even a good one) are generally not on one's priority list, and the back benches in those sessions seemed mighty comfortable.

My HR learnings come from my 25 years of global experience in management consulting, and from finding out the fact that, the one thing that has grayed my hair faster than my clients' has been the human resources challenges that come up time and again when Boards and CEOs effectively try to implement strategies.

I have seen too many CEOs and Boards challenged today by the human resources challenge, turning many of them into HR managers. And they have to deal with the problem in all the strategic and operational aspects of HR—from recruiting to retention.

I have also figured out that many of these CEOs just like me, may have also treated HR in business school the same way I did, or may not have attended to a business school at all. So, what I have tried to do is to write a simple book outlining the top 20–30 challenges that I see CEOs having to deal with everyday, and on a practical basis, what the solutions might be.

There is one more source of my knowledge about HR, Dr. K. K. Anand. He is a lot more qualified in this area—academically with a doctorate, and thought leadership in the subject in India. Many years of dining table conversations with him as he shared his management consulting experience in this area, and hopefully also a strong genetic link has also helped in shaping my understanding of the subject.

I'd like to thank Prriya Raj for a great set of illustrations that hopefully make the book fun to read.

Can't sign off without thanking my wife Monica, and my sons Sahil and Jai having tolerated me and my travel for all these years while I helped clients "unlock human capital."

Enjoy the ride.

Sanjiv Anand
Mumbai, August 2011

Contents

Part-I

Strategic Imperatives

1. The Board and Human Capital
2. Have CEOs Turned into HR Managers?
3. The Never-Ending Challenge of Work-Life Balance
4. The Real HR Stuff for CEOs
5. Structure and Musical Chairs—For Whom did the Music Stop?
6. Restructuring and Living to Tell the Story
7. Driving Enterprise Performance
8. Driving Individual Performance
9. Identify and Take Care of the Rock Stars!
10. A Stock Option Program that Works
11. Dealing with Cultural Diversity—A Unique Middle East Challenge
12. Strategic Project Management
13. Role of the Strategy Management Office
14. It is Lonely at the Top
15. HR Management in Family Businesses
16. HR Challenges in a Merger Situation

Chapter 1

The Board and Human Capital

I think we are all aware that many Boards of Directors often play a significantly expanded role in protecting shareholders' interests and also assisting management in making key decisions. Many of these decisions are focused on human capital management. There is a need for a board to balance its involvement in operational management, especially in the human capital area. So, where is the balance?

Selection of a CEO

Selection of a CEO is clearly an area within the purview of the board. There is a need to understand what kind of skills one is looking for in a prospective CEO. If the company needs significant internal transformation, then there is a need to get one who has strong operational management skills. On the other hand, if the focus is on growth and expansion, then one needs to pick the one who has a track record of driving enterprise growth, which may include experience in regional/international expansion. Nationality and industry background again are areas that need to be decided upon. My closing comment in this area: if you are using a headhunter, don't let him bully you. Most headhunters get testy if you reject their first list of candidates, which could often include an old lot that they are recycling. Force the issue and make sure they put a set of candidates on the table that suits your requirements, not theirs.

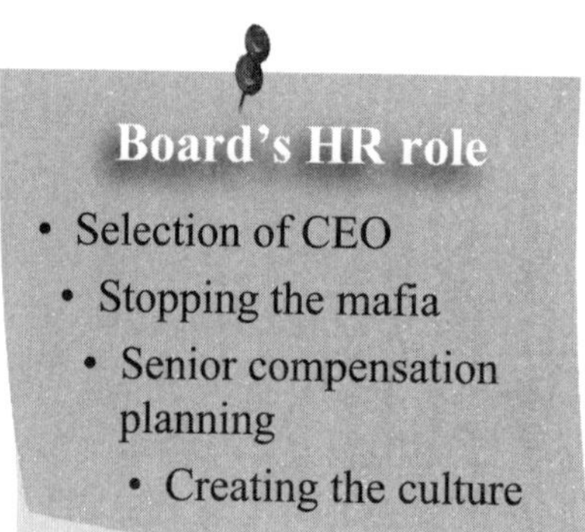

Stop the Mafia

In hiring CEOs, boards tend to encourage or allow the new CEO coming on board to bring along his/her 'mafia'. Generally, he insists on bringing along his ex-CFO (this makes it easier for him to massage the numbers) when he shows up, and then over the next one year, an entire gang shows up. Remember that the CEO is not your recruiter. It is better that he comes in alone and learns how to work with the existing management team, or brings in a new one that will be brought on board for the skills of the members, not because they know the CEO from his earlier tenure. Very often, boards allow the new CEO to bring in his ex-colleagues. The resulting problem is that it ruins the culture within the organisation, and when he leaves, all his buddies follow suit thus creating a bigger organisational void.

Compensation and ESOPs

The compensation of senior executives is key to recruitment and retention. In many situations, where it is hard to issue Employee Stock Options (ESOPs), the primary factor that will drive performance is variable compensation. While a good HR head will help you put into place a good fixed compensation structure, let the board determine the variable incentives to be paid, depending upon the performance it expects to extract from the organisation. For the right reasons, don't hesitate to pay 50–200% of fixed compensation, or 1–2% of profits as a performance bonus to get the results you want. And this principle not only applies to the CEO, but also the key executives.

Where one can issue stock options, the board must bring in an external advisor to design an ESOP program. Remember compensation has three components to it, fixed which is given to make sure people show up for work and do a reasonable job every day and variable, which ensures that annual profits/performance is delivered, and ESOPs to drive stock price. The ESOP process needs to be managed by the board to avoid conflict of interest.

Building an Organisational Culture

Everybody agrees that the customer is of paramount importance. But, what per cent of time at board meetings is focused on the customer? Statistics indicate, less than 20% of the time. If an organisation is looking towards building a 'customer-oriented culture', it needs to start at the top with the board. From there, the culture percolates down through the organisation in various ways—communicating the board's commitment to creating this culture to the workforce, creating a reward and recognition system such as 'Chairman's

Award' to recognise customer service and ensuring commitments to fund customer-oriented culture-building training within the organisation.

In the foreseeable future, I see many Asian and Middle East boards continuing to be involved in operational and strategic management. In light of this, playing the above role in the HR space is going to be critical not only from an HR perspective, but also to provide a framework for good governance in the organisation.

Chapter 2

Have CEOs Turned into HR Managers?

Thank you god and thank you boss ... for allocating resources to make our HR the best in the industry!

The Problem

The biggest complaint I have heard from my clients is that they are spending way too much time doing HR work and they hate it. They all understand that workforce management is important, and their involvement in it is with good intent, but it results in their getting sucked into it almost as a full-time job, and too often in a fire-fighting mode. So, what's going on?

It starts with a lack of real commitment to the HR function. With HR seen as a cost centre, the willingness to pay a top-notch HR Head handsomely is weak. The unwillingness to pay the price of employing a competent HR Head, and furthermore, the non-integration of the HR function/Head in the Executive Committee makes the situation even worse.

Absence of a good HR professional leads the organisation's CEO and business unit heads, who are generally more skilled in general management and operating specific business units, to play the role of HR Managers with limited understanding of the subject and without any relevant experience of the same. The amateurs then start to guess what the problem and its solution are thereby compounding the problem. In any case, they tend to end up dealing with HR administrative nitty gritty, which should have done by an HR-IT system, not even an HR Head. Add to this, in some parts of the world, the unique Asian and Middle Eastern managerial challenge when a Board of Directors, has often becomes de facto management by taking over, or rather interfering with a range of managerial responsibilities, including those of HR. And the damage is complete.

CEO's fix for HR

- Hire a great HR head.
- Sensitize the HR head to the business.
- Quantify expectations from HR.
- Reward for performance.
- Invest in a HRMS system.

What's the Fix?

The first obvious fix is to open your wallet, and go find an HR Head, who is suitable for your organisation. If your organisation doesn't have the basic HR framework in place, don't hire a HR guru or he/she will not last. Find somebody, who will last 24 months to get the basics in place, and then upgrade the HR function to its the next level. Don't attempt quick fixes by moving an internal non-HR person into HR position or promote a junior person into senior position just to fill the gap.

The next step after appointing the right HR Head is to sensitise him/her to the working of the organisation and its business, and the needs of the employees. Most professionals complain that the HR department is not responsive, and it takes a long time to get things done. Well, how many management professionals make the effort to update the HR team regularly with their business plans, operations, and let them know where during the course of the year, they will need HR help. Handing one sheet of paper to the HR team listing the top ten HR tasks for the year is a good starting point.

Quantify Annual Expectations from the HR

Complementing the above with critical performance metrics/expected turn-around-timelines will help quantify the expectations from HR. Take the top 10 HR activities and simply lay down the annual targets for each. For example, in the area of recruitment, estimate the number of strategic/non-strategic hires expected for the year, and the expected turn-around-time to fill those positions. You then obviously stick a serious performance bonus of achieving those targets. Remember it's almost a funnel effect. Removing the bottleneck in HR removes bottlenecks across the organisation. For the delay in the hiring of every sales guy results in revenue loss—avoiding this loss through timely recruitment is a benefit far more significant than the cost incurred in paying the HR team performance bonus.

Invest in HRMS Systems

Then one should invest in a cost-effective Human Resource Information Technology (HRIT)/Human Resource Management

System (HRMS). Almost all administrative HR functions, namely recruitment, leave management, payroll, etc., are automated, and maintained by each employee. Getting a CEO or for that matter HR senior staff involved in any of these functions is an utter waste of time.

What's been outlined above, if well executed, will take 90–120 days to get done. You are then ready to move to the real HR functions that the CEO has supposed to deal with—succession planning, variable compensation, ESOPs, talent management etc.

A closing comment for the HR professionals, who after reading this chapter are all of a sudden, feeling vindicated. In a recent CEO survey, 60% of them said that HR Heads are a waste of time! Oops! This shows that some of them may have to find a way of being better appreciated (and productive).

Chapter 3

The Never-Ending Challenge of Work-Life Balance

Over the years, I have heard senior executives complaining that they don't get enough time with their kids and family. Those moments with the family don't come back, and soon the kids go to college never to be back home as children ever again, and executives carry the regret of not having spent time with their kids for the rest of their lives. Here are a few simple and practical ideas to improve your work-life balance. This not only applies to the CEO, but across the organisation, as work-life balance has become an important issue, not only for the leadership team, but all employees. New generation of employees see this as important as their career development plans, and will often raise this issue with the leadership team and HR heads.

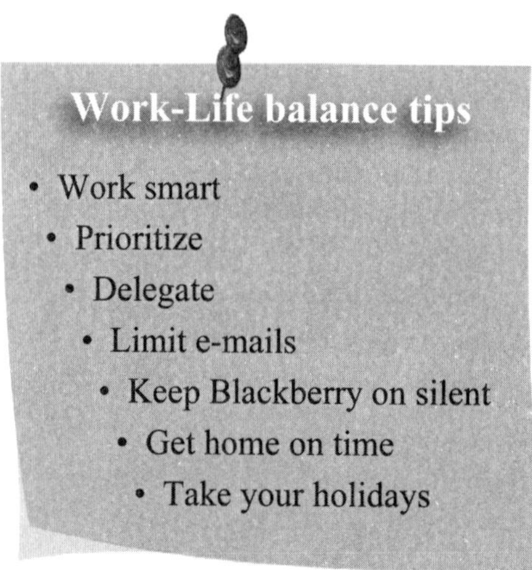

Working smart is the key. Simple things work. At the start of the day, create a to-do list: calls to make, e-mails to send, and the targets you need to achieve. Working through the list in an organised fashion and scratching off items completed, will give you a sense of satisfaction and also ensure that the work is done. More importantly, it induces some prioritisation. For those who complain that their schedules get hijacked by their bosses, my only response to that is, it depends on how much you allow it to be hijacked. Also remember to keep some time for yourself during the day. And definitely delegate what can be done at levels below yours. Doing a low-priority job yourself more efficiently than your junior does not make that activity a high-priority one.

Put discipline in an organisation—discourage copying all/many senior executives on e-mails. Be forceful about it. Not having read mails that you need not be reading, can easily save least 30 minutes in a day.

At a senior executive level, learn to work hard and smart during the working hours but make it a policy to get home just before dinner at least for your family and kids.

For those who travel, do it in a way that it does not destroy your health. Schedule flights so you can maximise evenings with the family. Also I have found rather than working on a flight, or reading a management book, just reading anything not related to management is a welcome break. A great novel will do. Also enjoy the hotel besides the room and the internet connection!

Protect Your Personal Time

Protect your weekends. In this area, the Americans, and even the Europeans do a great job. Unless you are an investment banker or consultant, everybody else shuts down work by Friday evening and focuses the weekend on family and the chores.

And most importantly take your full holiday quota. Here the Americans are lagging. Less than 50% are taking all their leave, and over 70% are checking their Blackberry's on leave. Nowadays it's hard to take 3–4 weeks at a time. Take a maximum of 2 weeks at a time, and then use the rest of the days during the balance part of the year to do short holidays. You will find yourself recharged over and over again.

Finally, what about your other wife—the Blackberry? Learn not to let it control you. When you get home, learn to shut it off, or in a worst case check mails a couple of time in the evening, rather than when the red light goes off every time. My kids taught me my lesson here. I kept complaining that they never sat and chatted with me at home till they said–what was the use since I was always checking my blackberry. I got the message.

You only live once. Make sure it's not only for the shareholder.

Chapter 4

The Real HR Stuff for CEOs

This is what I follow and my boss feels that I've all the leadership qualities!

In an earlier chapter, I discussed the need for CEOs to move away from being the HR managers, and focus on the real stuff. In this chapter, I will lay down the areas that a CEO should really focus on.

Structure

Business/organisational structure is the most critical HR component. At the end of the day, it needs to be aligned to driving business strategy—the CEO's core area of accountability. Often, management hands over the task of developing the structure to HR. However, HR's understanding of business is limited. It is, therefore, important that structural design be done by the CEO and the Executive Committee. The Executive Committee will include the HR Head. The HR Head's presence will ensure that the structure being decided by the management team will be in alignment with good HR principles: span of control, clarity in roles/responsibilities, best practices, etc. The CEO needs to ensure that the structures being designed are not individual-specific, but designed to drive business strategy.

Compensation

HR has a key role to play in deciding compensation, especially fixed salaries and allowances. However, today, increasingly the Board of Directors and CEOs are keen to build performance-driven organisations, and variability of compensation in relation to performance has become a critical part of compensation. While there are HR principles for variable compensation (e.g. 10% of fixed salary at the lowest level going up to even 200% of fixed at the highest level), at the end of the day, it's the CEO, who knows which executives or positions are key to driving strategy. Also, in a market-driven environment, it is possible that the pay of the best executives will not necessarily fit into the internal

- Structure
- Compensation
- Succession planning
- Creating a culture
- Communicating enterprise-wide

compensation structure, and that their compensation may need to meet market reality. Variable compensation is a way of meeting those expectations without destroying the overall compensation structure of an organisation which is, in any case, needed for over 90% of the employees.

'Hit-By-The-Bus-List'

This is an interesting way of looking at succession planning. While it is important to have succession planning for all positions within an organisation, there is what is a called a 'hit-by-the-bus-list'. This is a list of key positions whose executives, if don't show up to work the next morning, are likely to have an inordinately high negative impact on the business. The CEO needs to take into account the organisational structure, mark red the positions or people which/who are critical, and identify within the organisation those who can be the back-ups, who can potentially take those positions at a short notice. I know of a former Chief of Staff of the White House, who always kept such a list in his top drawer. Not a bad idea!

Culture

This is the hardest one of all. It is all soft and touchy feely, but has a real impact on the performance of the organisation. Often, CEOs have a tough time describing the organisational culture they have or the one they want. With a bit of prodding, the common terms they come up with are **'performance-oriented culture'**, **'sales-oriented culture',** and **'customer-oriented culture'** etc. Irrespective of what one finally decides about the culture of the organisation, culture is a function of behaviour and behaviour starts at the top. The reality in business is: **'what is important for the boss is important to me'.** So, if the CEO shows attributes of functioning along the lines of the work culture he or she is interested in and recognises, or rewards similar behaviour among the employees within the organisation, the culture of the organisation will move in the same direction.

Lastly, let's learn to communicate. Leadership starts at the top. How about making the effort of walking across all departments of the organisation once a month, standing there, and spending

10 minutes giving everybody a first-hand feel of your and the organisation's priorities, and answering questions. This concept of 'town hall' meetings, well used by the US Presidential candidates, is often used by a large number of CEOs in the US. It works wonders. While it won't make you the US President, it will bring you closer to your organisation and will initiate in you, the making of a good, if not a great leader.

Chapter 5

Structure and Musical Chairs—For Whom did the Music Stop?

Yes, we've got the ideal structure and perfect strategy. What I do is to keep fiddling with the two to justify my authority and position!

Organisational structure creates strong and often contradictory perceptions. Everybody recognises the need for the right organisational structure, but often, people think that the structure comes in the way of getting things done effectively. The problem lies elsewhere.

It is quite clear that structure follows strategy. And alignment between strategy and structure needs to be strong. While the business/strategy should be the starting point of building the right structure, what happens is that boxes get drawn around individuals to accommodate their personal aspirations rather than what is right for the organisation. If the board challenges the CEO on this issue, the defense is that it would be hard to find a replacement. However, no business is unique and nobody is indispensable.

Control the Number of Direct Reports

The additional challenge facing CEOs is the number of direct reports. I've seen them go up to 15. It is physically impossible for a CEO to respond to or keep track of that many direct reports, especially in high growth markets; 8–10 is a good number.

Getting structure right

- Align to strategy
- Don't build boxes around people
- Limit direct reports to 10
- Create SBUs
- Avoid matrix structures
- Change only when necessary

Today, to get the number of direct reports under control, a firm appoints a Chief of Corporate Services to whom heads of HR, Finance, IT, etc., report. Though this can be an innovative approach to easing the burden on the CEO, a word of caution: availability of people with an understanding of all of these areas is limited. Anyway, it's still worth a try. The SBUs may ask the board/CEO to include support staff within their SBUs, so that things don't slow down within the business unit. These positions can then have a dual reporting to functional heads.

Create SBUs

Creating Strategic Business Units (SBUs) is very important, especially in the Asia/Middle East region. Most firms in the region tend to have a range of diverse businesses, with limited synergy. From a legal perspective, while they may all belong to the same parent firm, operationally they are quiet different. Therefore, creating SBUs, and then empowering and holding accountable the GM for the P&L of that unit, is essential. This also implies the need to provide authority, something that the board is hesitant to do. My view is to be fair about it.

Overcome the Challenge of Matrix Structures

This brings up the issue of matrix structures. As we are all aware, matrix structures create dual reporting. For example, the head of investment banking of a leading bank would not only report to the country head, but also to the regional investment banking head. This is to ensure geographic and product alignment. My general experience has been that it requires significant maturity for management to understand the concept of two bosses, and very few employees know how to make it work. They tend to play one boss against the other. So, the next time you get tempted to draw many dotted lines in your structure, think again.

About 20 years ago, while I worked as a consultant in the US, I did a lot of work for AT&T. In every meeting I went to, I was amused when shown organisational charts which were as recent as three months old, but then I was told, they were already outdated! There is a strong message here. As long as there is no act of god, and no significant change in the business, don't play with the structure, i.e. do not reshuffle the functional distribution/arrangement. It may be wise to consider changes at the beginning of each year, but don't overdo it. Otherwise, people will forget where in this game of musical chairs, they all need to sit!

Chapter 6

Restructuring and Living to Tell the Story

I planned to write it as a short story but with its twists, turns, angles and tangles, the company restructuring plan has become an epic!

This is the kind of experience that can grey your hair quickly. It doesn't win you popularity contest. The benefits are not immediate. The rumor mills can often undermine your objectives. The bottom line is it's not for the faint hearted. I have been fortunate to have led a number of restructuring operations over the years, and am still living to tell the story.

Do it Surgically

There are a number of ways to execute this operation. My style is to do it quickly and surgically. First, to reiterate, structure follows strategy, and any transformation needs to be driven by a board/CEO approved way forward strategy. Furthermore, since new structures result in role-changes, getting the management team to approve them is inappropriate–they will have a conflict of interest. It's all very well to say that they will take a corporate/impartial view of it–that's theoretical. They tend to very much look at it from their own perspective, and also think of the structure in context of the existing strategy and processes. The closest you will get to an impartial reviewer of new structure is the board, and potentially the CEO.

Also, the CEO often has to be reminded to wear the corporate hat, and not be swayed by his close colleagues within the management team. HR should also be involved at the appropriate point. Once the CEO/Board put together the plan, let the HR head have a look at it and provide comments. Once the plan is finalised, the HR head will have to play a significant role in its execution–identification of employees, issuing of letters, handling exits, realigning compensation if required, assisting in communication, etc.

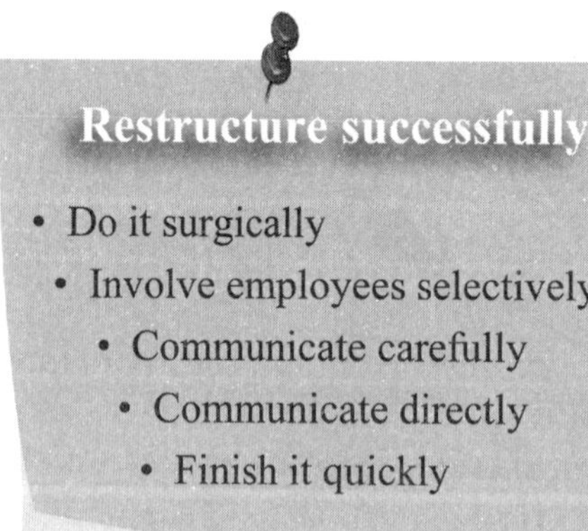

Communicate the Change Carefully

There is always a pressure to announce the change to the larger audience. The CEO will be bombarded with questions, and people will get nervous. My view is that you only communicate when you are clear about what you want to communicate and to whom. Those who are performing well are never nervous. The ones who are nervous tend to be ones who are unsure of their performance, and they need to be nervous. The first presentation to the senior management team should be a summary of the strategy. This gives the team the context to the organisational change that is about to come. I have debuted a new structure to a broader management forum-hell tends to break loose, and people immediately start jockeying to secure positions.

Give the Message Personally

After briefing the team on the strategy, a set of one-on-one meetings needs to be conducted with those to be assigned new roles. HR gives them a letter confirming their new position. Also have their new job description ready and a presentation outlining the role and strategy of the unit/role they are about to take over. These meetings need to be back-to-back and finished over a couple of days, and as much as possible the new position should be taken over within 4–7 days of being handed the confirmation letter. Also preferably, the more done on the same day, the better. People will also say that they need more time to execute the handover. My view is that any critical parts of the handover should happen immediately; the rest can happen when the person is in the new role. After all he/she hasn't left the organisation. On the day of the handover, make sure you set up a help desk, so that the employees can walk over and ask questions/clarifications once in the new position. Without delay, targets need to be provided for the new position, and potential incentive plans should be announced for those employees who most effectively facilitate the organisational change.

The above works well where you are not cutting headcount. Restructuring with a headcount reduction–well, that's another story. Get your helmets on, it's a story for another day!

Chapter 7

Driving Enterprise Performance

Organisations are keen to become strategy-focussed and drive enterprise and individual performance. Very often, management asks HR to create Key Performance Indicators (KPIs) to drive individual performance. Prior to developing Individual Performance Measures (IPMs), it is critical to develop an Enterprise Performance Management system (EPM) so that IPMs are aligned to strategy. The world's no. 1 EPM tool is the **Balanced Scorecard (BSC)**. How does it work?

It is critical to first identify the top 20–25 financial customer processes, and organisational and IT objectives that the firm wants to focus on. This is the cockpit view of the strategy—the dashboard. Organisations often lack focus on executing strategy. This forces them to prioritise and identify the most important financial and non-financial objectives they need to deliver on.

Then comes the critical aspect of measurement—identifying performance measures to determine success in delivering the strategy. Measures can be lead or lag. Most financial measures are lag. You only know how well you have done after the event/quarter is over. For example, quarterly earnings is a lag measure—can't be fixed once the quarter is over. It is therefore important to create lead measures. A good example is frequency of customer meetings. The assumption is more the meetings, the higher likelihood that the organisation will meet its financial targets. The selection of measures is key to driving individual performance. If the sales team is in a position to meet its targets by selling more to existing customers, then the measurement and target of sales to existing customers becomes critical. Don't attempt to institute too many measures. 25–30 measures will suffice.

Ownership as Targets

Just as one needs to have exam grades, one needs to set targets for the measures selected. Many organisations set too many aggressive targets stretching the limits of organisational capacity, or not having or allocating enough resources to deliver the targets. Often, I have found that setting 4–6 aggressive targets is adequate to implement the strategy. If you focus and you push hard enough on those, you are likely to achieve the desired results. Also, remember to keep some easy targets. For example, in a year of organisational transformation, one is not likely to get high employee satisfaction.

Identifying owners for the key strategic objectives is a critical step in focusing enterprise performance at the executive committee level. Key members of the executive committee need to take ownership of effectively implementing strategy. Very often, these areas will be within their operational control, and they will be responsible for them in any case. Also, they may be asked to look after objectives that may not be under their operational control, but which are important for the organisation.

Lastly, inventory the projects running in the organisation and align them to the strategic objectives. Projects are invested in to effectively execute strategy. Projects that cannot be seen as assisting in driving enterprise performance are questionable and could be dropped.

In conclusion, I would like to re-emphasise the following–unless there is clarity on enterprise direction, creating aligned individual performance measures will be difficult. Remember not to incentivise for delivering the wrong objectives, or the strategy will remain where it normally gets stuck, as another confidential document on an executive shelf!

ILLUSTRATIVE: BALANCED SCORECARD STRATEGY MAP

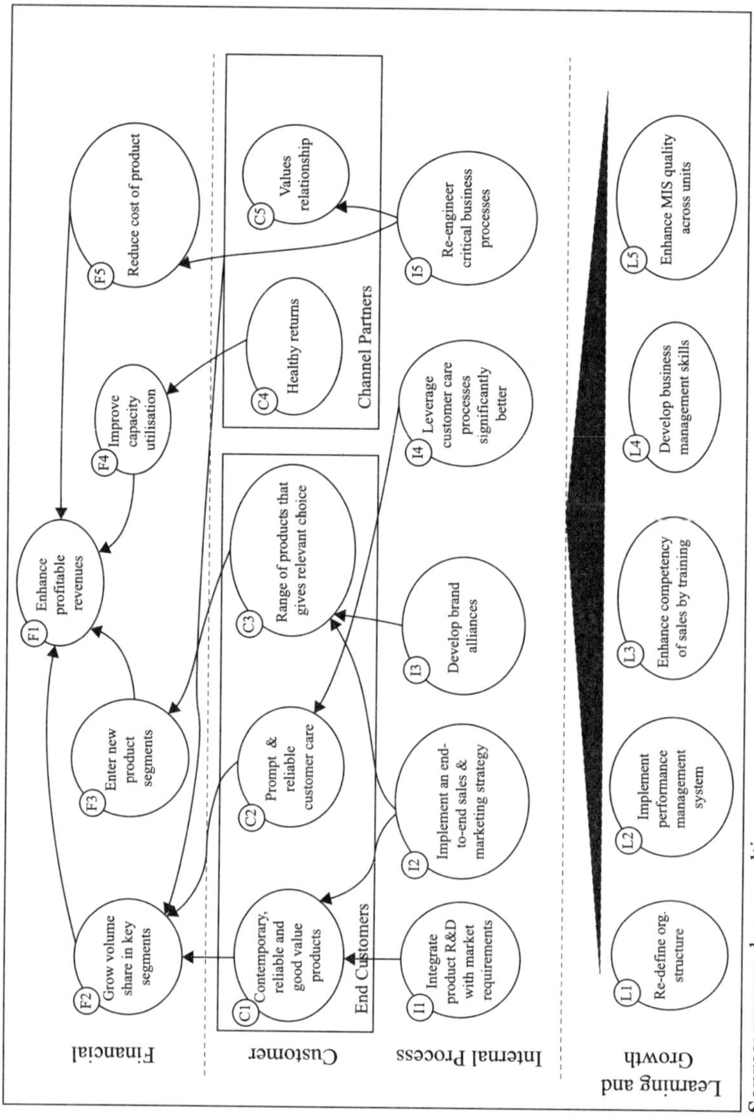

Source: www.cedar-consulting.com

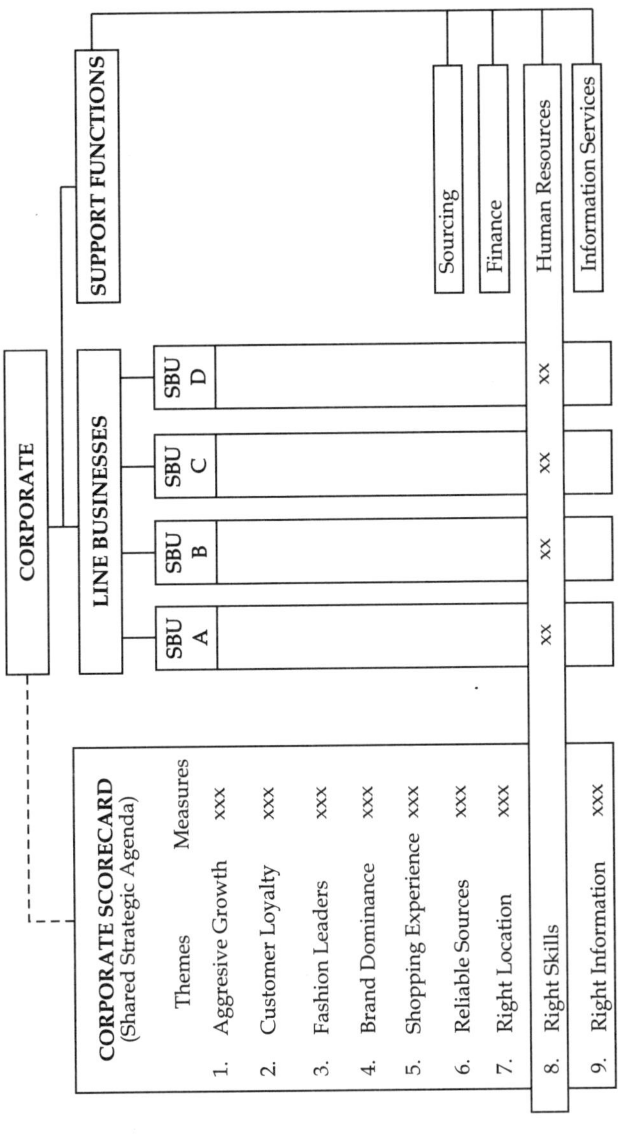

Each SBU develops a Long-Range Plan & Scorecard consistent with Corporate Strategic Agenda

Each support function develops a plan for "best practice" sharing to create synergies across SBUs

Source: www.cedar-consulting.com

BALANCED SCORECARD: ABRIDGED SNAPSHOT

Objective		Owners	Measure	Target	Actuals
Financial	Enhance profitable revenues	CEO	Growth in revenues & EBIDTA	10%, 15%	
	Improve capacity utilisation	GMM	Growth in % utilisation	80%	
	Reduce cost of product	GMM	Cost reduction from current base	50 Million	
Customer	Contemporary, reliable & good value products	GM Sales	Brand image rating	4 on 5	
	Prompt & reliable customer care	GM Sales	Customer service rating	4 on 5	
	Healthy returns	CFO	ROI > defined minimum	30% +	
Internal	Integrate product R&D with market requirements	R&D	Reduction in field rejections	100 ppm	
	Implement an end-to-end sales & marketing strategy	GM Sales	Market share	25%	
	Re-engineer critical processes	GM Ops	# SLAs agreed	20	
Learning and Growth	Re-define organisational structure	GM HR	# of defined positions	40	
	Implement performance management system	GM HR	# of positions with KRAs	40	
	Enhance MIS quality acorss units	IT Head	# of standard MIS formats	20	

Source: www.cedar-consulting.com

ILLUSTRATIVE LIST OF PROJECTS

<table>
<tr><th>S. No.</th><th>Area</th><th>Projects</th></tr>
<tr><td>P1</td><td>Finance</td><td>New Pricing Structure (AUM-based Advisory Fee) on Mutual Fund</td></tr>
<tr><td>P2</td><td rowspan="5">Customer / Markets</td><td>New PMS Proposition</td></tr>
<tr><td>P3</td><td>Improved Customer Welcome Kit</td></tr>
<tr><td>P4</td><td>Design & Conduct Customer Satisfaction Survey</td></tr>
<tr><td>P5</td><td>Launch Brand building campaign</td></tr>
<tr><td>P6</td><td>Undertake Market Assessment of Competitive Product Landscape</td></tr>
<tr><td>P7</td><td rowspan="2">Process</td><td>Auto Generation of Client Statement & Automation of Client Reporting</td></tr>
<tr><td>P8</td><td>Document PWM Compliance and Risk Manual</td></tr>
<tr><td>P9</td><td rowspan="5">Organisation and IT</td><td>Organise Professional Training Programs for Relationship Managers</td></tr>
<tr><td>P10</td><td>Design & Conduct Employee Satisfaction Survey</td></tr>
<tr><td>P11</td><td>Implementation of Sugar CRM</td></tr>
<tr><td>P12</td><td>Implementation of Online WMS</td></tr>
<tr><td>P13</td><td>Revamp Website</td></tr>
</table>

Source: www.cedar-consulting.com

Chapter 8

Driving Individual Performance

Remember the Tom Cruise movie, where he's a sports agent, and the guy he's representing reminds him what's important. In high-growth markets, finding good resources is difficult, and cutting a fixed paycheck isn't enough anymore. This looks like you have to turn into Tom Cruise (not a bad option!), and learn how to respond to employees' expectations nowadays. They may not be as vocal as Tom's client, but the thoughts are the same. Loud and clear—show me the money!

It is therefore essential to add a strong annual component of variable compensation based on the performance record of meeting specific targets. The concept is not new. For years, KPIs, KRAs, MBOs have existed. But their importance today is greater, especially with their link to compensation. Surveys indicate that employees place 60% importance on compensation, and the balance on hygiene factors. In the Middle East/Asia, the 60% can rise to 75%, so let's get it right.

Position	Individual Performance Measures (IPMs)	Measure Weightage	Target	Actual
Relationship Manager	Segment growth-current portfolio	30%		
	Lead generation-new account revenue	35%		
	Cross-selling revenues-within current base	25%		
	Customer satisfaction-feedback	10%		

Source: www.cedar-consulting.com

Designing good Individual Performance Measures (IPMs) starts with the issue of what to measure. As I indicated in an earlier chapter, it is important to have clarity on the way forward strategy, and if you have built an Enterprise Performance Measurement System/Balanced Scorecard, you should be quite clear on what the top 30–40 strategic corporate objectives are. Use them as a reference framework, combined with operational responsibilities, to identify key measures of individual performance. Remember the most important factor here is that you must measure an individual's performance on factors directly under his/her control. Often, I've seen corporate profit as the primary criterion for measuring the performance of employees. That is too generic and a person's performance often cannot directly relate to profit or drive it. So, it is better to have a measure specific to a person's area of responsibility.

How many measures does one need? No more than 4–6. I have seen companies trying to measure employees on 15–20 measures. This approach never works. When a firm finds it hard to meet four different targets consistently, how can one expect an employee to do so? Also, HR should evenly divide the measures between the perspectives: customer, financial, process, organisational, and IT.

The next issue is the relative importance, or weightage, of the measures in terms of the organisation's strategy and goals and the person's role. So, if increasing profits is the key to the organisation's business, I would not hesitate to put 35% weightage on that, on the CEO's IPMs. If maximising sales to existing customers is the key, then on this measure, the same logic would apply.

Setting targets on these measures becomes an issue. There is always a tendency to play with the target number: the employee wants to make it easy to achieve, and the employer, more difficult. I can only say that the best thing is to do it in an honest way. If two out of the 4–6 targets need to be challenging, make them challenging, but support the employee if he needs corporate assistance to deliver those.

Measuring people correctly

- Identify 4–6 measures
- Weigh them correctly
- Set targets carefully
- Create a mix of difficult and easy targets
- Focus on direct control factors
- Pay for performance

My last word on this is that you should make sure that it is **easy for the employee to understand** all targets and objectives, and that at the end of the day you can accurately measure the inputs. And let the money at the end of the IPM rainbow be real for employees—at least 15% of fixed compensation at the junior level—going up to even 200% plus for the CEO for successful performance. If you show employees the money to drive performance, meeting the same expectation from shareholders will be easy.

Chapter 9

Identify and Take Care of the Rock Stars!

Our business draws a lot of inspiration from your business. Here's our weekly list of top 10 ... Our top 10 performers for the week!

Employees in all organisations perform at different levels, based on their motivation, experience and competency. When performance reviews take place, managers have to rate their employees in a manner that they fit the bell curve: 20% poor to average performers, 60–70% good performers, and around 20% in the excellent category. If the performance evaluation is done correctly, then the identified 20% excellent performers can drive the overall performance of the organisation.

However, even amongst these top 20% employees, there will be a select group of those who have performed exceptionally well and have the potential to shoulder greater responsibilities with relatively fewer years of experience. These are the 'Rock Stars' who need to be identified and nurtured. These are usually young employees, who have performed exceeding well and consistently in the last couple of years, are willing to take on additional responsibilities, can act with greater maturity, and have a burning desire to excel. HR along with managers of the concerned departments can identify these employees and put them on a fast track career path.

Nurturing these employees and grooming them to become responsible leaders is extremely important. These employees tend to be very enthusiastic and may leave the organisation, if they do not see themselves moving up fast in their career. Hence, it may be important to communicate to them that they have been identified as having high potential and that they would be groomed accordingly. However, to ensure that they do not take things for granted, inform them that their performance will be monitored regularly to ensure that they meet the organisation's expectations.

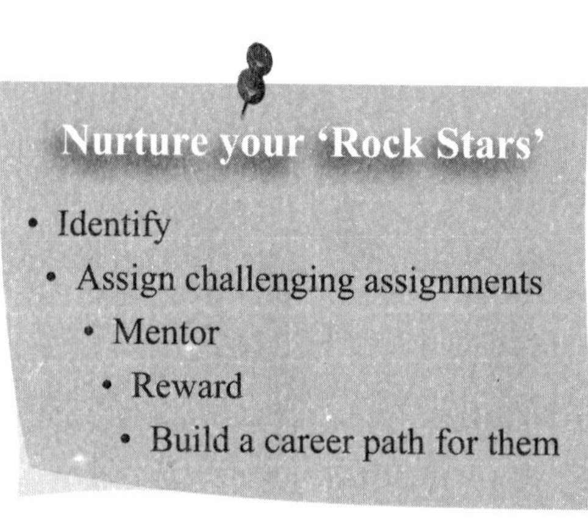

For the identified employees with high potential, develop a fast track career path. If possible, move them across various functions over the next couple of years, so they understand the working and complexities of the complete organisation. Give them stretch targets and special projects to work on, so their performance can be tracked. This will also help management to validate whether the identified high performer is performing consistently in high pressure situations. Through periodic performance evaluation, identify areas of improvement that these candidates need to focus on. If necessary, send them for development and training programs, wherein they can pick up the necessary skill sets they lack.

Another area to look at is mentorship of these employees. Identify key managers in the organisation, who themselves have been high performers and who can be looked up to as role models. Assign these mentors to the star performers to provide the necessary advice and guidance.

Rewards in terms of compensation for fast-track employees, is generally not different from the regular compensation structure that the organisation follows. Having different compensation structures will create dissonance across the organisation. However, by virtue of being identified as a fast track employee, a person in expected to rise higher in the organisational hierarchy at a faster pace than his/her peers. Hence, the compensation and rewards will be commensurate with the new position the person is promoted to, based on performance.

Having avenues for fast-track career path in an organisation is a great motivator, especially for high-performing young employees. It also creates a succession pipeline for the organisation, and most importantly motivates other employees to improve their own performance to get on the fast-track wagon.

Chapter 10

A Stock Option Program that Works

Your future performance is now firmly linked with the performance of the company ... on the stock exchange—with this stock option!

As organisations become increasingly performance-oriented, it is essential that a 'pay-for-performance' culture be created. The two components of pay that are largely accepted are fixed and variable compensation (increasingly better understood). Fixed compensation generally ensures that an employee does a reasonable job. Variable compensation focuses on meeting annual revenue/profit goals. Now the time has come to focus on the most critical aspect of an organisation's reason to operate—its stock price, and the need to incentivise its employees to help improve shareholder value.

Employee Stock Option Programs (ESOPs) have been around for years, especially in the US, and thousands of millionaires have been created as a result of it. Silicon Valley thrives because of it, and globally it is a common compensation tool used to help drive enterprise stock price performance (though generally the link cannot be made directly and publicly). At its core, the value of an ESOP program is that it helps drive performance, improve retention of key employees, and attract good ones. However, just having ESOPs is not enough; you have to have the right program. And at the heart of that comes the program design that needs to effectively answer the following questions—whom to give, how much to give, and when to give?

The Design

In the past, options have been given to every employee. This has not really worked. The reality is that the junior employees are fungible resources, who are replaceable (sorry to burst somebody's bubble here.). Therefore, nowadays the focus is on **giving the senior management**, and some of the middle management, ESOPs. This is an 'inverted pyramid model'—more stock options for the top of the organisational pyramid, and some/none for the bottom of the pyramid.

How much to give? Well, the financial industry blokes have always been generously awarded in terms of compensation, so why should the party stop here. Financial services, and high-growth industries generally target a 5–7 times CTC (cost-to-company) as the total options to be issued to an individual they are targeting. More mature manufacturing industries growing at less than 10% a year give about twice the CTC. The general idea is to make the quantum large enough to make it attractive. Remember that there is a circuit-breaker here. In most countries, the total amount of options issued should not exceed more than five per cent of the capital base. Remember stock options are not free (unlike restricted stock). The price at which it is to be issued is the most recent stock price or based on a recognised valuation model. This is the price the employee pays when he sells his vested shares, and pockets the difference, assuming the price of the shares has gone up when he can sell them.

A great ESOP program

- Focused on middle and senior management
  - 2X to 5X CTC
    - Vesting over 4 years
      - Options allocated on performance and criticality

This brings up the issue of **when to give**? Generally ESOPs work better for listed companies as the stock is more liquid and value is clear. Also vesting is done over a 4–5 year period. It means that if one has been issued options, one can sell those options over a four-year period at a certain predetermined rate (e.g. 25% a year)

As more and more companies are getting listed, especially in the Middle East and Asia where there is an increasing focus on improving liquidity of stock exchanges by encouraging family and government businesses to list themselves, using ESOPs as a compensation and performance driver will no longer be an option, but a necessity.

Chapter 11

Dealing with Cultural Diversity—A Unique Middle East Challenge

The designer seems to have lifted the idea from us. We also deal with the cultural diversity issue in our organisation with a mix and match policy!

In the Middle East, where 60%+ of the population is expatriate in many countries, the ethnic employee profile looks like a mini UN. They are from different religions and countries with diverse cultural, political and economic experiences. Therefore, it would be no surprise that their view of their employer, and of the future opportunities will vary. Even in organisations when there is minimal or no cultural diversity, there is a significant challenge to get everybody aligned to the company's strategy to focus in one direction—the challenge in the Middle East gets even greater.

Before dealing with the cultural diversity within the organisation, in the recruiting process itself it needs to be taken into consideration. While the decision should be based on merit, it is important that in the recruiting process, diversity should be encouraged and be balanced. The first preference should go to a national for obvious reasons, but if the skill sets are missing then an expatriate needs to be hired. Balancing nationalities is important. For example, most or all of those who directly report to CEO should not be of one nationality. Even within one division, there should be cultural diversity. Also in the recruiting process, it is important for the HR department to normalise or calibrate educational qualifications of the candidates from the different countries. For example, 90% grade of one country's education system may be equal to 75% of another country's.

Then arises the issue of educating and creating sensitivity about different cultures. Currently none is being done at all. To start with, one needs to educate the new recruits or employees on the country they are working in. If it is the UAE, then all incoming employees within the UAE must be educated on economic, socio-economic, and religious cultural issues. Learning Arabic over the second year of employment must be encouraged and funded by the firm.

Following that, one has to take a look at the most common nationality that works within the organisation and 10–20 information packs on each country need to be created and put on the company intranet site. Along with that it is important that one of the employees from one country make a presentation on that country. Combining this with the celebration, or at least, announcement of the key social/national/religious events of those countries will help.

All of the above strategies are effective in creating cultural sensitivity. The reason why all of this is being done is to drive individual and corporate performance at the end of the day. Here, I believe it is important to recognise the professional strengths and weaknesses of each nationality and leverage the former. For example, if employees of a certain nationality can speak Arabic which is crucial in key roles such as relationship management with certain customers, the employees of that nationality should be better leveraged in Arabic-speaking areas. If employees of certain other nationalities bring strong analytical skills, then using those skills in relevant positions should be used.

This is not about discriminating against any particular nationality. In India, 70% of the Indian software professionals are from South India. For years in the US, Chinese and Indian professionals have formed significant percentage of the research and development teams at Bell Labs, and other research organisations. It is about chess and checkers. A few years ago, I read an article that all employees are different, more like chess pieces rather than checkers where all are the same.

The challenge is to win the game using their different strengths rather than turning them all into checkers!

Chapter 12

Strategic Project Management

I think I've been evaluated on absolutely wrong measures—missing of deadlines and messing up of projects!

From my experience, 60% of a company's projects/initiatives fail or are not completed on time. Considering the time, energy and money, companies put into projects, these statistics are disappointing. There are a number of reasons for failure. But, let's begin with a few simple reasons.

Firstly, people are **never clear what a project means**. Often, operational activity is considered a project. For example, adding new customers in a year is not a project, it is an operational activity. Setting up a new plant, a new business, a new IT system are some examples of projects. A simple definition of a project is something that has dedicated people and financial resources, and has to be completed in a certain timeframe.

Then comes up the issue of figuring out what is the **current list** of ongoing projects. Unfortunately, in my 25 years of consulting experience across the globe, I am yet to find an organisation that has a handy list of ongoing projects. It is also important to recognise that at the end of the day, projects are done to help implement strategy. It is therefore critical that all existing projects and projects with the potential to be taken up in the future are mapped to strategy to ensure they will add value, and that a firm is not carrying out projects just for the sake of doing them.

Now comes the important issue of **sponsorship and staffing**. Unfortunately, this is a fact of business life: what is important to the boss is important to me. Therefore, it is essential that the projects have senior executive sponsorship. Two or three key projects must have the sponsorship of the CEO. These are obviously the ones that can provide an inordinately high benefit to the organisation in terms of cost or revenue. Then, the next in line to CEO must at least take the role of sponsoring 1–2 projects and be held accountable for

Great project management

- Define what is a project
- List
- Prioritise
- Create ownership
- Track progress
- Reward success

their success–both from a career development and compensation standpoint. Projects should be allocated to them based on their area of strategic responsibility as there is a direct link between the benefits of the project and the implementation of their strategies. This also creates accountability: if the strategic objectives can get delivered without the project getting completed on time, then why did they sponsor or recommend the project in the first place?

Let's not confuse the role of a sponsor with that of the **project manager**. The project manager is the one who has the responsibility of completing a project and managing it on a day-to-day basis. Often, significant errors are made here in selecting the project manager, and in my view, at least 50% of project failures is due to such errors. For example, having a project manager on a new project who has just come off a failed project and has low credibility, is a case of bad selection. Similarly, selecting internal auditors to run projects is another instance of bad selection—who wants to talk to internal auditor! So, pick the right person—somebody who is bright and a future leader. Lastly, the team under the project manager needs to be clearly identified. They don't have to be full time, but their roles need to be clearly defined, and they need to be incentivised for the success of the project.

Nobody has ever got fired for messing up a project. Maybe it's time to put into practice some of the above, and hold people accountable.

PROJECT MANAGEMENT TEMPLATE

<table>
<tr><td colspan="4">ABC</td></tr>
<tr><td>Workstream</td><td colspan="2"></td><td>Sponsor</td></tr>
<tr><td>Purpose</td><td colspan="2"></td><td>XXX</td></tr>
<tr><td rowspan="2">Dedicated Financial Resources</td><td colspan="2" rowspan="2"></td><td>Project Manager</td></tr>
<tr><td>XXX</td></tr>
<tr><td rowspan="2">Dedicated People Resources</td><td colspan="2" rowspan="2"></td><td>Priority</td></tr>
<tr><td>A, B, C
(A-High, B-Medium, C-Low)</td></tr>
<tr><td>Supports the Strategic objectives:</td><td colspan="3"></td></tr>
<tr><td>Benefits</td><td colspan="3"></td></tr>
<tr><td>Schedule / Milestones:</td><td colspan="3"></td></tr>
<tr><td>Start Dates:</td><td colspan="3"></td></tr>
<tr><td>Key Activities</td><td></td><td>Key Milestone:</td><td></td></tr>
<tr><td>Key Activities</td><td></td><td>Key Milestone:</td><td></td></tr>
<tr><td>Key Activities</td><td></td><td>Key Milestone:</td><td></td></tr>
<tr><td>Key Activities</td><td></td><td>Key Milestone:</td><td></td></tr>
<tr><td>Completion date:</td><td colspan="3"></td></tr>
<tr><td>Dependencies:</td><td colspan="3"></td></tr>
</table>

Source: www.cedar-consulting.com

PROJECT STATUS REPORT

Project	ID	Spsr.	Proj. Mgr.	Start Date	End Date	Status/Issues/ Next Steps	Invest.	Benefit	Budgeted Y/N

Source: www.cedar-consulting.com

Chapter 13

Role of the Strategy Management Office

In a competitive world, all recognise that they need to be **'Strategic-Focused Organisations (SFOs)'** to succeed. But, the key question is: where does the role of strategic planning sit, and how must it be configured to make the strategy most effective?

The tendency has been to assign the responsibility of strategic planning to the CFO, with the assumption that the finance department knows all the numbers and a good understanding of the organisation. However, the finance department often has a great understanding of the numbers, but not what drives them from a product, process, organisational and IT perspective. Therefore, in my view strategic planning needs to sit nice and tight right next to the CEO.

SMO framework

- Reports to CEO
- Manages strategic planning
- Manages projects
- Budget alignment and MIS
- Six-member team

Organisations that have got this approach right have generally put a senior strategic planner in the role. However, with organisations and markets becoming complex, it is not possible for an individual to address both the market and functional complexities. Therefore, in my view, the function of strategic planning needs to be entrusted to a team, or a **strategy management office (SMO)**, rather than to an individual.

So, what is the role of an SMO? It should focus on the following—assist in the development and roll out of the corporate and divisional strategy in alignment with the budget, produce executive-level MIS (Management Information System) to facilitate strategic decision making, co-ordinate executive committee meetings, map the external environment for new businesses including M&A (merger and acquisition) opportunities and changes in the demand and competition for existing businesses, work with external consultants on strategic projects, and prepare strategic presentations for the board, internal and external audiences. All of this makes it obvious that it is not a one person's job.

The SMO can have 3–6 team members depending upon the size of the organisation and the number of divisions. I would structure it in a way whereby one part of the team is focused on tracking the external environment, another part on assessing the internal performance of the organisation at a strategic level, and a third one on developing and reporting strategic MIS/EIS (Executive Information Systems).

The question I am asked often is what are the **skills required by the SMO team**? Strategic thinking does not come naturally to most, and the SMO is not to be a dumping ground of operational executives for whom no operational role can be found. I think it is a good idea to hire a management consultant who is tired of traveling and wants to improve work-life balance to head the team. Under him/her there needs to be a team that has some operational experience, extremely strong analytical ability and communication skills. Less arrogance of being close to the king will help! And a reasonable level of maturity is required so that others within the organisation feel that the team has operational experience and therefore is credible.

I have not spoken about using the office as a Project Management Office (PMO) from where all strategic projects can be mandated and monitored. There is a possibility of integrating the PMO into the SMO.

Less than 15% that can formulate strategy execute successfully. Let the SMO improve your chances of success, so that implementing your best strategy has better odds than a lottery!

Chapter 14

It is Lonely at the Top

For all the benefits and recognition that a CEO gets, the one that gets taken away is the ability to talk relatively openly to others within an organisation. There is no peer left to talk to, talking to an immediate subordinate on confidential matters carries risk, and talking to a board member can potentially jeopardise job security. So, it is lonely at the top. However, there may be a few solutions to this solitary confinement.

Let us first **look inside the organisation**. There are likely to be a couple of direct reportees that you as the CEO can trust significantly and feel comfortable talking to. However, lack of comfort with the board, your own compensation, and your intent of looking out for alternate employment are not topics to be discussed with them. They can primarily be used as sounding boards about the organisations performance and strategy and selective inputs on a few individuals. This has to be done carefully and privately so that the others do not get a sense of a 'mafia' like situation. And with the first whiff about these individuals using the conversations for personal benefit, or bragging about closeness to you, these conversations need to be ended.

What about **board members?** Well, it depends. If you are new to the organisation, it is risky. Boards in the Middle East and Asia are more operational, and many of the members have personal relationships that extend outside the board, and many that you may not be privy too. Therefore, tread with caution. However, over a period of time, you will find select board members who are willing to build a strong personal and professional relationship. Use this relationship carefully and ethically as a genuine sounding board, but not to play politics, especially between board members. That will come back to bite.

The best sounding board internally is a board member if the relationship is used ethically, with no political agenda.

Consultants and advisors, can often be good sounding boards, but remember they may not be permanently around. I sometimes also play this role. However, one needs to be sure that the consultant is providing guidance on a confidential and ethical basis, and will not misuse the information. Also, you need to be sure that the consultant has the 'executive coaching' skills besides the functional and operational skills. Most importantly, the advisor needs to be a good listener.

What about personal **friends** outside the organisation? To be honest, it generally has not worked. They may be great friends personally, but may have limited expertise and understanding of your business or role, and their advice can actually cause more harm than good. And confidentiality is at serious risk. Pillow talk will ensure it is shared the same evening, and then from that point, *it will beat Chinese whispers in terms of speed and accuracy.*

However, there are interesting **external** options. Recognising that CEOs do need a sounding board, a number of organisations like the Young President's Organisation (YPO) and a number of others, offer a number of forums that offer confidential sharing and feedback. These need to be explored.

I am sorry; I have not been able to provide an ideal solution. Unfortunately, one would have to play it by ear!

Chapter 15

HR Management in Family Businesses

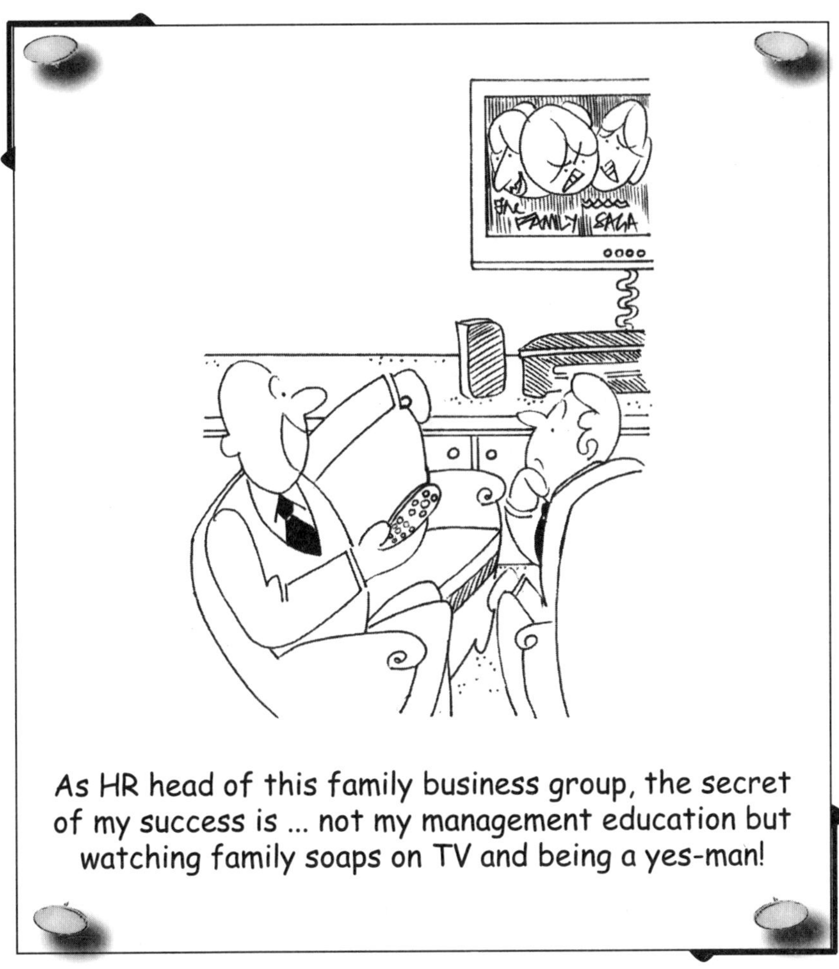

As HR head of this family business group, the secret of my success is ... not my management education but watching family soaps on TV and being a yes-man!

Eighty per cent of the companies around the world are family-owned. So, unless you plan to work on another planet there are eight out of ten chances that you will end up working in a family-owned business. The biggest complaint about family-owned businesses is that they are not professionally managed. The response of family members is that all professionals are not equally competent, and that family members have greater concern as their financial well-being is at stake. This argument can never be settled. The answer is somewhere in between family-owned/family-managed and family-owned/professionally-managed. Either way, the HR professionals get stuck between a rock and a hard place, trying to find the balance. This chapter is to help the shareholders deal with this issue, and the HR brave hearts so that the HR function can be progressive, and family-owned organisations are able to retain the right people.

From a **shareholder's perspective**, the existing family members in the business need to have their roles clearly defined. Employees cannot have three bosses to report to with e-mails being copied to everybody. Some family members are not interested in operational responsibilities. Keep them on the board so they have an oversight and can protect their shareholding. Some like to work for 50% of their time. Stick them to management oversight committees that oversee businesses with management once a month. Pick businesses in their area of interest. This is a semi-board like role. Then there are family members who want to be operationally involved. Let them incubate new businesses (subject to board approval of the business plan) or run an existing business. My view is if they are willing to work hard, have the right attitude, the appropriate education, and 60%+ of the skills required, let them professionally run it. To cover the skill gap, simply ensure their next in line are excellent.

Eighty percent of the global businesses are family-owned. Unless you are planning to leave the planet, learn to make the relationship work.

For the **young guns who want to join the business**, many families globally have set standards on who can join, at what level, and many are often not allowed to join. In Asia and Middle East, the culture is different. People run businesses not only for financial reasons, but because of family tradition, social standing, etc. My view is young family members should be allowed to join business as long as they have the right education and the right attitude. Skills will be taught in the company. The assignment should be based not only on competency but also on personal interest. In the internet age, if the young family member wants to start an internet company, with the right business plan and management support, he or she should be allowed to incubate.

The **HR Head** in a family-owned business has to have a strong personality with seniority in experience and age and be able to speak up, and speak his mind before family members and the board. Remember the movie *Godfather*? He or she needs to be something like a consigliore (a trusted advisor). Also, the HR Head should be able to dissuade family members from being feudal—handing out bonuses outside policy, hiring family members and friends for the wrong reasons, taking the professional management for granted, etc. In fact, my suggestion is to make things simple, as much as possible—automate the HR function so that it is hard to manipulate, for both family and non-family members. Other than that I recommend implementation of HR policies just as in any professional organisation. And hold your ground! No one said it would be easy.

You would be surprised how many family members would appreciate an honest HR advisor, rather than a yes man—whose availability is unlimited, and has a skill set that even a fifth grader possesses.

Chapter 16

HR Challenges in a Merger Situation

He saves his job everytime the company is acquired by someone—not because he is always the best man but because he manages the new boss so well!

For all those who thought that their firm was being merged, here is a quick word of caution. It is generally an acquisition, and if your firm is at the receiving end of the transaction, forget all the press announcements. Statements like 'merger of equals' are for public consumption. The reality is more like the law of the jungle. From an HR perspective, the dominating firm will seek to dominate all key positions in the combined entity. And unfortunately for most positions, **there can be only one person.**

In the case of pure acquisitions, the firm that is doing the acquisition generally wants to ensure a rapid alignment of operations. There can be no blockers. In the case of a large MNC firm doing acquisitions, as soon as the transaction is completed, they fly in with a team that within the first month has to determine the culture and the attitude of the senior management team. Those that are seen as blockers are let go. Bottom line is that the senior management is expected to be positive change agents so that the integration can be rapid and successful.

The situation gets more interesting when two entities are merging their businesses. One will dominate as outlined above. In a merger, **alignment is required from a financial, product, customer, process, organisational and IT perspective.** The organisational one is the trickiest for obvious reasons. The starting point is to look at the broad strategic direction of the combined business. Also, another pertinent question is whether the merger is done from a growth perspective or a cost synergy perspective. If it is from a cost perspective, then there is an obvious mandate for serious headcount reduction besides the need to address other HR alignment issues.

Based on the combined strategic direction, a **quick review of the structure** needs to be done to allow for phase 1 alignment. The critical positions are one down to CEO. The correct position to take is: the best man wins. However, an individual should not be looked at in isolation. If an individual from company A is excellent and the department he has to run is better in company B, then there is a real question about A running a department that somebody else set up, and the acceptance of that individual. So sometimes, decisions need to be taken keeping in mind the divisions of the organisation that individuals are about to run.

There is obviously a need to align job descriptions, compensation, HR policy and all other key HR processes. An HR integration team can be put together roping in business unit representatives to drive the integration process.

Irrespective of whether the merger is for reasons of cost-cutting or not, the reality is that **the merged entity will end up with excess headcount.** Shareholders are comfortable with having excess headcount on the revenue generating side. The logic is that it will help grow the business. The issue is with the excess headcount in support and operations. Here, there is a definite intent to cut cost as you do not want duplicates for the same positions. **Unfortunately politics rather than process tend to win.**

Dynamics in a merger

- Be a positive change agent
- Remove blockers
- Align business processes and IT
- Align structure
- Remove excess headcount
- Merger of 'equals' is a myth

There is no real good news in this note. If you are part of a firm that is going through an M&A, there will be blood on the street, and the best man does not always win!

Part-II

Operational Stuff

17. An HR Department that Works!
18. Developing an HR Scorecard
19. Can Manpower Planning Work?
20. Innovative Fix for Hiring Challenges
21. Mentoring—Does It Sound Greek?
22. The Nightmare Called Training
23. I Just Called to Say Hello!
24. Taking Care of Happy Campers
25. Having a Great Off-site
26. Employee Ethics and Responsibilities
27. Setting up Your Firm's Oscars
28. Effective Sales Force Compensation
29. Managing Employee Exits

Chapter 17

An HR Department that Works!

That's nothing! Our HR guys can play not just a double role but four roles with superb action!

In many surveys, CEOs often indicate that their HR departments are a waste of time, that their HR heads are slow moving and theoretical and do not live in the real world, and that they do not understand how to align HR in the delivery of strategy. Thus, this chapter is to help my HR friends in winning back some credibility and adding greater value within the organisation.

HR strategy needs to follow enterprise strategy. So it clear that the HR department needs to understand what is the company's strategy for the next 24–48 months. Is the financial strategy a growth strategy or driven towards cost containment? Is the customer strategy about accessing new markets/adding products or leveraging the existing relationships and expertise better? Is the process strategy about innovation or improving efficiency? And what will be the HR and technological framework to support the above process, customer, and finally financial strategy'?

Following this approach, one can determine the key 10–20 HR objectives/initiatives for the year, and the performance measures. For example, if the delivery of the above strategy is dependent on recruiting 15 new people with key skills on a timely basis, then that becomes a key HR objective. The bottom line here is that HR deliverables should drive employee commitment that in turns drives customer commitment leading to investor results.

There is also the market context to keep in mind. For example, companies are changing continuously and seeking to create learning organisations. Management styles are changing to matrix management and multi-skilling. Also globalisation trends imply the need for organisations to work seamlessly across borders, and drives the need for mobility of employees.

Roles

HR can broadly function in four roles–*Change Makers, Regulators, Advisors, and Hand Maidens.* The first two are interventionist in nature, and Change makers and Advisors are strategic in nature.

The **Change Maker** role focuses on areas such as realigning structures, becoming internal change agents, active board engagement, defining and monitoring competencies and intelligent resource planning.

The **Advisor** role is more focused towards coaching, development of new management styles, internal training, maximising opportunities for career development within the organisation, internal communication, and creating the right organisational culture.

The **Regulator** role is what it sounds like–setting of policy, contracts development, and compliance.

And then there are the **Hand Maiden's**. This HR focus is around automating key HR processes such as pay and pension, recruitment, contracts, and benefits administration. In addition, areas such as employer assisted programs (such as stress counseling), and facilitating visibility of individual skills/knowledge and experience.

At the end of the day, as outlined earlier, HR departments need to show to the CEO and the business units to whom they are service providers, and finally the shareholders, that what HR is doing is bringing a demonstrable impact on business results. And understanding the business strategy, mapping HR roles in delivering this strategy, measuring its performance, and clearly determining which of the above four roles outlined is the primary role it is seeking to play will go a long way in justifying its pay check! For HR itself! Wow, that would be something.

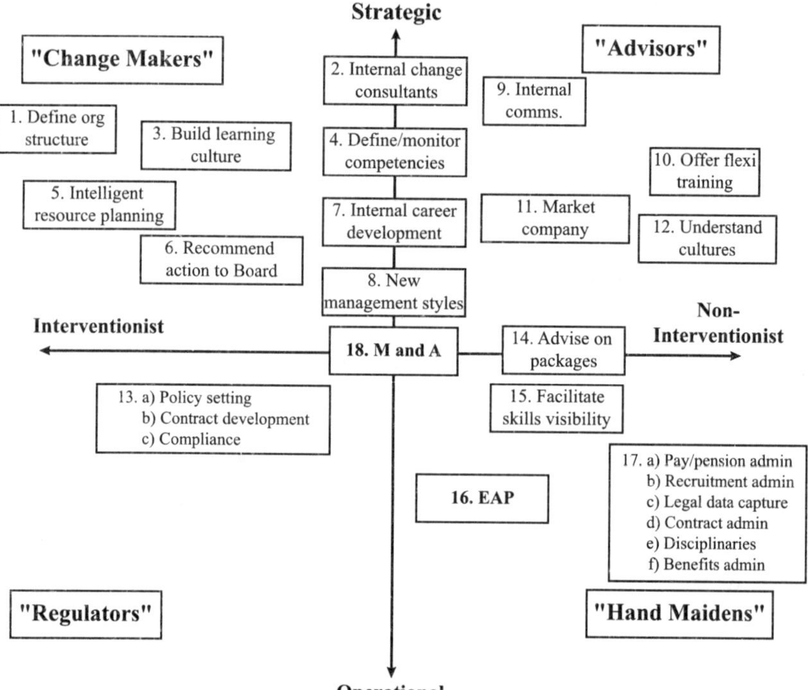

Source: www.cedar-consulting.com

Chapter 18

Developing an HR Scorecard

In keeping with the spirit of making the HR function more valuable and effective for organisations, I will focus this discussion around the development of an HR Scorecard.

The HR Scorecard is built on the principle of the Balanced Scorecard. It's a cockpit view of a department/company. In the HR context, building an HR scorecard will help determine what are the top 20–25 HR objectives that an HR department needs to focus on, what are the performance measures and targets to achieve those objectives and what are the top 10–15 projects that need to be done to deliver the organisation's strategic objectives.

Since the HR department is not a revenue generator, the **top most perspective for an HR department's scorecard is meeting internal customer expectations**. Customers from an HR perspective could be Unions, Employees, Line Managers, and Senior Management. What are the key customer expectations that the HR department needs to meet during the course of the year? They could be around managing career planning, compensation, training and skills development, etc.

The **second perspective is financial**. In order to meet the above customer expectations, what are the key financial objectives that an HR department could have? These could be around meeting its own internal HR Budgets, ensuring that compensation and manpower budgets are on target, and also potentially ensuring that the IT system investments in HR have resulted in the efficiency gains.

In order to meet customer and financial expectations, HR like any other department needs to **excel at key processes**. There could be 50 processes within HR, but from an organisations standpoint no more than 20% may be mission critical. The idea is to identify those and ensure they are excelled at. These could be recruiting, performance appraisal, change management, etc. It depends where in the company is its current lifecycle.

Lastly, in order to excel at key process, the HR department itself needs to have the right **human capital framework and technology**. Human capital framework includes the right structure, clarity in roles and responsibilities, compensation, competencies, and the appropriate system of rewards and recognition. On the technology side, over 80% of HR transactions are administrative in nature and there are multiple IT systems available to automate those functions.

Once the HR head has identified the top 20–25 HR objectives using the above framework it is important to identify 20–25 performance measures to track HR performance. While HR tries to make employees performance, target oriented, it very often fails to recognise that it has the same responsibilities for itself. Reporting performance once a month to senior management helps clearly demonstrate performance of the HR organisation.

In the Middle East and Asia, finding high quality HR professionals is always a challenge. By putting a HR scorecard together, one at least ensures that the HR team is all focused in delivering commonly identified objectives. This at least ensures that an average quality department delivers significant value.

While the HR will never be a revenue generator, by building a performance oriented HR organisation, it will ensure that the revenue drivers in the organisation have the right support to drive enterprise financial performance. And for once, HR will not be considered to be theoretical and blue sky oriented, but a true support organisation.

ILLUSTRATIVE: HR STRATEGY MAP
Customer
Financial
Internal Processes
Learning & Growth
C1 HR provides timely, qualified resources
C2 HR ensures optimal compensation plans to improve retention & motivation
C3 HR creates a proactive and engaged culture to support my unit
C4 HR staff are accessible and promptly respond to my queries
F1 Benchmark and optimise HR costs
F2 Make selective investments to track and improve HR services
Innovation
Operational Excellence
Service Quality
I1 Implement enhanced/ custom compensation plans to reduce employee turnover (especially field)
I2 Ensure performance culture, aligned to corporate goals
I3 Ensure timely recruitment especially key positions
I4 Continuously map and enhance competency
I5 Streamline HR processes and customer service
L1 Improve HR staff skill sets and cross training
L2 Right size staffing to provide improved service levels
L3 Implement technology to enhance core HR processes
L4 Enhance work culture and performance management

Chapter 19

Can Manpower Planning Work?

On my flight back from Italy recently, I saw an Economist report that said that after Saudi Arabia, the UAE had the second highest middle/senior management compensation on the planet. Compensation in the Asian region has also gone through the roof. Whether this encourages you to look at how many you hire, or load your organisation, the reality is that for any organisation to succeed, its cost structure needs to be optimised, and that means carefully managing your manpower.

The reality is that if you talk to any senior HR professional, they will tell you that manpower planning is not working. At the start of the year, most departments make no serious effort of analysing manpower and productivity, and during the year they will ask for additions without any significant justification. Here are a few ideas today to make it work better.

At the **core of this is structure and the underlying activity**. When structures are designed, positions are often created for activities/sub-activities, without really analysing whether there is enough work for one person in that area. For example, saying I need one product manager for every product sounds logical, but if the activities will only take 25% of his time, then it is only logical that the person handle 3–4 products. So my first recommendation, is that when structures and positions are created, think about the level of underlying activity before drawing some of the boxes.

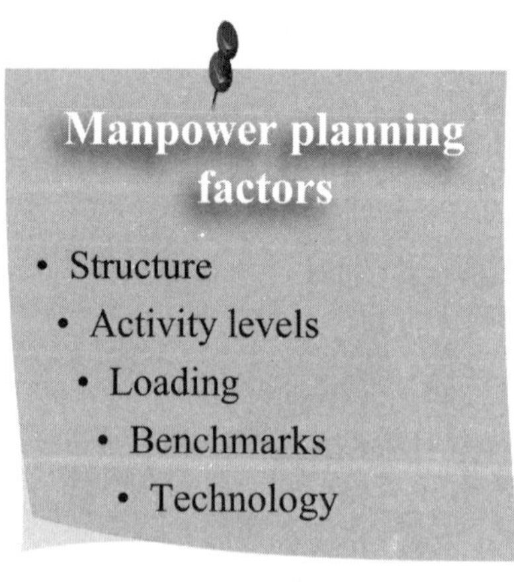

Then arises the **real issue of loading**. It is critical that one understands detailed activity levels to determine the number of people needed for each position. A quick look at the headcount by department is the starting point. If 70%+ of the headcount is not customer facing, one has to wonder what all these people are doing. After all, isn't the role of a company to generate sales, and for every sales guy, if there are six people in support, common sense tells you something is wrong. It gets even worse when these people are in administrative positions.

Activities and loading for most of positions are well understood today. There are plenty of **benchmarks available** to determine what the right loading/staffing is. Very often benchmarks can be internal. If a firm has ten branches, and the average sales call of branch 1 are 15/day and the other branch is 6/day, you have a right to go back to the second branch productivity/loading improvement.

Technology can also play an important role. In many organisations where we are determining what is the right size of the organisation, we will look at the current role of technology and see how it can improve productivity. After all, processes are done by people enabled by technology. To be fair, one must compute loading prior to technology upgrade, and post-upgrade.

A few years ago, I had a client of mine ask me to run all the analysis, improve the productivity of the organisation, and then asked me to put the benchmark of optimum loading per position on one sheet of paper that he kept in his drawer. Every time somebody came to him asking for more staff, he simply used the reference loading template, to determine if additional staff was needed or not. A good round of analysis, some benchmarking, and single sheet of paper can go a long way in determine if your organisation is right sized, and the only flab you need to worry about is what's on your stomach.

Chapter 20

Innovative Fix for Hiring Challenges

The growth of certain economies has created a recruiting challenge. The resulting situation is a **resourcing nightmare.** Many positions are vacant. To fill those positions, juniors with missing skills are being promoted. If a position is taken to market, the headhunters are not able to deliver due to lack of effort or lack of availability. So what's the solution? Not an easy one, but worth a shot.

Firstly, **segregate positions** that should be handled by Board/CEO, and those by HR/CEO. Simple thumb rule–CEO and direct reports to be recruited by CEO and Board, and remaining by HR and CEO.

Now if a slot opens up, the first place to **look is inside, but in a structured way**. Job post the position internally, and allow candidates from any department to apply. Since this is sensitive as the existing employee may not want his boss to know, let him apply directly to HR in confidence. HR can then look at the candidate logically, and then follow it up with an interview. If the first round interview goes well, HR can then involve the target department and the department the employee could be exiting from to take it further. HR can position it in a way that the candidate did not necessarily apply for the slot, but as part of the resourcing process HR is responsible to see if there are resources internally that can fit the vacant position, and believes the fit is strong. A senior executive/CEO can get involved to make a strategic call that it is in the organisations interest to move the person. Remember, filling positions internally does not only come from job postings. HR in any case should be looking at internal inventory of people.

Strategic recruiting

- Identify key positions
- Source internally first
- Use recruiters externally
- Don't panic and hire the wrong person internally or externally

If an internal replacement is not available, **open the position to market**. Again, I have a thumb rule here. If the position is a

CEO or CEO direct report, give it to a head hunter on retainer. The headhunter will be more dedicated. Be clear on what you are looking for, and don't let the headhunter force you into accepting candidates so it makes their job easy. Also select the headhunter carefully. Do their reference checks, and ensure they have experience in the same function or industries. Plan for the process to last 90 days.

If it is a position below the CEO direct reports, you may be able to **use a recruiter** who works on a success fee basis. My understanding is that because of the volumes, internal research teams of recruiters are not spending more than 6 days looking at internal databases and short listing candidates. If they don't have one on database, they give up, but they won't tell you that. The solution is build a strategic relationship with two recruiters, let them search in parallel, and give them some kind of fixed fee at the start of the year as a commitment that can be adjusted against fees during the years as positions fill. This will increase commitment. A **fix and variable fee model**. Innovative, but should work.

I don't guarantee you still won't get grey hair recruiting, but hopefully it will stop you from going bald!

Chapter 21

Mentoring—Does it Sound Greek?

Enlightened HR managers and companies often consider implementing a mentoring program. A quick question first. Where does the word 'mentor' come from? In Greek mythology, Ulysses asked a close friend Mentor to guide and take care of his son, while he was away in battle. From its mythical origins, the word 'mentor' has come to mean someone who guides a junior. Well, so much for the trivia.

Mentoring programs in a firm are not for everyone but mostly for new joinees, newly promoted leaders, and those with a responsibility for strategic projects. These programs need the sponsorship of the CEO to succeed. Start them on a small scale, and then grow them as they become more credible.

The most common question we often come across is **what the roles of a mentor and mentee,** are in a mentoring program. The mentor's role is to be the sounding board for the employee, remain apolitical, help the employee to understand the organisational culture, keep all conversations confidential, leverage internal personal networks to help the employee succeed and provide feedback for employee's personal and professional success.

What about the **'mentee'?** He/she needs to be a good listener and take feedback positively, use the opportunity to the fullest and in good faith, not to leverage the mentor politically, keep the conversation confidential, take responsibility for his/her actions, and invest time and effort in fostering the professional relationship.

The CEO and HR department typically **match a mentor to a mentee**, i.e. avoid having both of them from the same department to minimise the risk of political undertones/actions. One must set about trying to identify potential mentors. Obviously, those who have good listening skills, have been in the organisation for a reasonable time, understand the organisational systems and are generally regarded as successful. While having seniors in this role is good, it is not essential. All seniors do not necessarily have these skills.

Successful mentor-mentee interactions don't happen on their own. HR should clearly communicate the roles and benefits of a mentoring program. Also, it is better that the mentor and mentee meet at least once a month outside the office, preferably for lunch. Moreover these programs need to be reviewed periodically to see how they are faring. Review them in annual forums and seek ideas for improvement from the organisation.

Benefits

At the end of the day, one assumes that there is a benefit to the firm for running a successful mentoring program. The Centre for Creative Leadership in the US found that 77% of the firms running these programs reported improved retention rate. Additionally, a poll of 378 US firms also showed that those firms used mentoring to enhance career development, leadership skills, and put candidates with high potential on the career fast track.

The observations that we have made today are no rocket science. It is obvious that in any sphere of life, whether at personal, professional, or even at the CEO's level, it is always good to have someone to talk to—someone who is willing to listen, and give honest advice. That is what mentoring program does for an employee. And it is not something that a boss can do, or for that matter a spouse.

Seventy per cent of the firms that used a mentoring program reported improved retention rate.

Chapter 22

The Nightmare Called Training

How many times have I heard CEOs and employees say that training is a waste of time, never benefitted from it, that the effectiveness of the training was never tested, that many missed sessions, or even worse—most sat in the back row and slept post lunch. So, is training really a waste of effort? It depends whether an employee is training for the sake of training or is serious about it. That depends on whether the executive committee is willing to get involved, or just leave it to the HR to use its own limited judgment. Let's start at the beginning.

Firstly, I believe that **training can only do so much for you**. What I mean is that if a person has 60–70% of the required skills, it can add 10–15% more, to make him more productive. But if the person has only 50% of the competency required for the job, then training won't work. This is truer, the higher you go in the organisation. Therefore the fix numero uno to the training nightmare is **recruiting the right guys for the right slots.**

- Source people correctly
- Train seven days a year
- Both internal and external
- International training for seniors
- Do not waste time on measuring effectiveness

Then, let's move to how **much training is needed?** The IT consulting industry estimates 12 man days of training per year—50% self-learning, and 50% classroom-learning. Figure out what works for your industry. For the sake of simplicity, my general view is seven days of training a year is enough, five in classroom, and two on one's own. Many training programs are week-long, so that's perfect time span. Alternatively, it can be split into two programs.

The big issue is **what to train for?** Let me try to simplify it again. Senior management (CEO and immediate subordinates) needs to go for leadership and general management programs. They often end up attending industry-specific programs. That is acceptable once in a while, but I would rather prefer them to be speakers at industry programs than be participants. Middle management needs to attend specific functional programs, like leadership and coaching programs, or industry programs. Junior managements need to focus on its functions, and vocation/personal skills.

Then how about **location of training**? Las Vegas, everybody? Doubt it. Unfortunately, the junior employees most often end up in training sessions organised onsite, or at a location close by. Middle management should train off-site and potentially in another country. **Senior management must be internationally trained**. I am a strong believer in this. When one trains senior management in the same country, the person often learns nothing significantly new from the participants or faculty. However, when they are sent overseas, the learning comes from participants and internationally exposed faculty. At some of the best business schools in the US, a three-day program costs only $5000.

And **who is sent**? Once you set the thumb rule, everybody goes unless somebody is on probation, or about to be fired. HR with the Executive Committee can prepare a list of programs, literally as a menu that an employee can select from with the mentoring/approval of his boss. **It is hard to measure effectiveness,** so my recommendation is not bother too much about it. More important is the debriefing after the employee returns, and asking him to share his experience with others in writing or in presentations.

As long as the training program is designed along the above lines, value addition to employees and the company is guaranteed, and priceless.

Chapter 23

I Just Called to Say Hello!

On the other hand, when I communicate as a CEO—whether in a meeting or a seminar or in a conference—everyone is made to listen or else their salary is slashed!

In the era of telecommunications, where interaction outside the office has reached peak levels, within organisations communication still leaves a lot to be desired. People are operating in silos and even in the silo, adequate communication is not happening top-down.

We all agree that we want to create strategy-focused organisations. In order to do so, one needs to be able to **communicate strategy across the organisation**. This makes communication even more critical. The original complaint about the lack of communication of strategy was that the strategy document was like the key to the executive washroom: the document stayed with the executive committee, but the management that had the responsibility to implement strategy had no clue what to implement because nobody bothered to communicate it to them. I have also seen other extremes. On a visit to a French client, I entered the boardroom and found on all walls, slides pasted from the strategy report. I asked the CEO what was going on. His response was that since he wanted to communicate the strategy to the workers—he had them walk through the boardroom every 15 days and read the slides on the wall—almost like a visit to an art gallery! I am not so sure if this was the best way to do it. Anyway, this just emphasises the point that while people recognise communication as important, they are unsure about how to communicate.

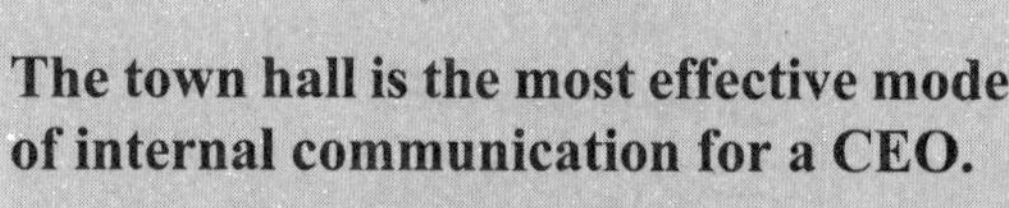
The town hall is the most effective mode of internal communication for a CEO.

There are three ways to communicate—build formal forums, create formal communication channels, and raise the level of informal group verbal interaction.

Channels

The formal forums are critical. There should be a bare minimum two of them—one at the executive committee level (CEO and his immediate subordinates), and one at the departmental level (Department head and his immediate subordinates). The departmental-level meeting should be a weekly operations committee meeting. The executive committee meeting can be bimonthly and follow the basic ground rules to ensure a good meeting—time span of not more than an hour or so, clear agenda, focused discussion, and circulation of output documents before the meeting. The purpose of these meetings is simple—to report what has happened so far this month, year-to-date, what does the rest of the month and quarter look like, and what does the management need to fix collectively together so that the organisation stays on target. Through these forums, executives have an opportunity to collectively inform and decide rather than being done one-on-one with the left hand not knowing what the right hand is doing.

The formal communication channel is about effectively using the organisation's intranet capability and nowadays even social media like facebook and linkedin are being used for the same. An internal newsletter can be put up once a month combined with at least one letter from the CEO, and another letter and profile of a senior executive. This, combined with some personal, social and community networking capability on the site to ensure that the people go to the site, places the organisation in the reasonable first stage of an internal communications framework using the net.

To conclude, I go back to the 'Town Hall' concept I discussed earlier in the book. Nothing works better than the CEO walking around and stopping at various departments and delivering a ten-minute update on the state of the business, and answering questions and shaking a few hands. Direct communication from the guy who should have a sign at his desk that says **'the buck stops here'** will do wonders to an organisation's morale and focus on strategy.

Chapter 24

Taking Care of Happy Campers

Here's the proof that our people are highly motivated and highly enthusiastic. We monitor their levels at the time-check everyday in the morning!

When an employee wakes up in the morning, and looks forward to going to work, it's the simplest sign of a motivated employee. Many look at this the other way around, looking at who is willing to work late as a reflection of employee motivation. **I look at it at the start of the day, not at the end of the day.**

Everybody is well aware of the need for employees to be motivated. Well-directed and motivated employees drive enterprise performance. The topic has been analysed extensively, and in many companies, a range of coffees in a company cafeteria have been credited with helping drive employee's motivation! If a company has to rely on coffee selection for motivation, then unfortunately the basics have gone missing. In my view, it is relatively simple with 3–4 simple drivers.

Fifty to sixty per cent of the motivation comes from compensation, and the right compensation is a mix between the fixed and the variable. It is the variable compensation that drives the individual to compete and perform. The review of compensation/ performance done fairly on an annual basis includes looking at compensation packages across the organisation and outside. I don't think that employees expect the employer to be the best pay master, but at least a competitive one.

The **next motivation-driver is who you work for, and who you work with**. If you respect your boss, and have a good working relationship, that's another 30% of credit on the motivation side. What makes a good working relationship is a topic in itself. However, I would simply summarise it as: a good boss is the one who leads from the front, is honest, hard working, willing to listen but at the end of the day will lead and take the easy and tough decisions, who operates on the basis of fairness, who is not abusive, who is willing to empower and provide authority, and ultimately rewards and recognises success.

Depending upon the level within the organisation, **medium to long-term career** opportunities contribute to another 10–20%. To be honest, too much is made of this. Very few employees have the ability to appreciate the medium to long-term career opportunities. I have stayed with the same employer for 22 years; very few have similar kind of patience. The minority of employees who do is easily recognisable and operates with an entrepreneur's mindset rather than an employee's. In any case, what gives them kicks is quite different from what motivates a regular employee.

And the final 10%, I would put to what we all call **hygiene factors** such as physical work environment, HR administration. This used to be important a few years ago, but this aspect is so well understood and fixable with small investments that most companies have taken care of this.

Motivation-drivers

- 50% Compensation
- 20% Working relationships
- 20% Career opportunities
- 10% Hygiene factors

Just as I indicated at the start of the article, I had a very simple test of how one feels about work every morning as a good indication of motivation. There's another simple one at the end of a year—even better than an employee satisfaction survey. If at the end of year, an employee looks at his résumé and he/she believes that not only has value been added to the organisation, but to his/her own professional track records, then we are sure we have a motivated employee with us, another happy camper!

Chapter 25

Having a Great Off-site

We were in Singapore recently for our own mid-year offsite. By the way, a great place to hold an off-site. I think it went well, but I need to wait for the employee feedback on it. Clients often ask us, if we could help them with an off-site or provide some advice. Companies spend good money on it, and want to make sure it goes well.

It all starts with **determining the purpose**. Is it a team-building exercise, is it a development of next year's strategy, a mid-year review, a major corporate event discussion such as a integration of an acquisition, or a sales planning exercise? The purpose needs to be clear as it determines audience, ambience and content.

Figure out **who you want to take along**. This depends upon the above and the size of the organisation. Planning exercise should be limited to the CEO and his first line reports, and in some cases their one downs. Unless it is a team-building exercise for a wider organisation and the organisation is small, restrict the group. Carefully identifying the group also allows one to pick more interesting locations. Today, for a limited amount of money, you can get anywhere on the planet. Don't be extravagant, but don't let the budget also be a constraint. However it should not exceed 5–6 hours of travel. Self-contained resorts with some sightseeing close-by are great options. Shopping locations are a bad idea—people get dispersed and there is no bonding. The length generally should be two night/three days for a major off-site or two nights/two days for a mid-year or smaller off-site.

What make a great off-site?

- Define its purpose
- Who goes?
- Master of ceremonies
- Icebreakers
- Corporate games
- External resources
- Time to bond

You need to find an **internal master of ceremonies**—somebody who is good at organising, has some seniority, and is somewhat of an entertaining character. Let him work with the secretarial staff and the travel agencies to pull the event together. It makes all the difference.

At the start of the sessions, there need to be ice-breakers. C**orporate game** books have plenty of ideas. The starting one should last no more than 45 minutes so that you can soon get down to work. The program during the day needs to be clearly laid out. Maybe the main session should be addressed by the CEO, and then have smaller sessions providing multiple people opportunity to present. Makes it less boring and creates involvement and interaction. Keep an eye on the clock, and if discussions are becoming operational or moving off the agenda, let them be taken off-line.

Often, clients ask if they should take an **external resource.** This is generally a good idea, but it depends on the intent. If it is for team building, then the resource can organise corporate games for you after about 4 pm in the afternoon after you have had your day work sessions. If you believe that you need a resource to facilitate your work sessions and decision making, then there are resources available for that–typically corporate trainers. Generally a good idea but don't let them hijack the event. Make sure they are briefed correctly and they don't take all the airtime.

Leave enough time for **relaxation and bonding** outside the work session. And lastly don't bring the spouses along unless you are planning to turn it into the biggest political event you have ever organised!

Chapter 26

Employee Ethics and Responsibilities

I have talked about the responsibilities that organisations have towards their shareholders and their employees. Today, in the world of hop on and hop off, it's time to **remind employees about their ethical and fiduciary responsibilities towards their employers.**

The first and most important factor is to learn to **honor your commitments**, whether at work or at home. **You cannot have two different standards**. When you join a firm, you are not seeking part time employment. Companies hire full time employees so that they provide security and career opportunities in exchange for your commitment to add value to an employer. If an employee leaves within three years, the employee has not been fair to the organisation. The first year goes in learning the business. Only over the next two years is one able to add value. By not staying through the two additional years, one has not given enough time to the employer to assess your progress and provide you growth and promotion opportunities. By not having patience, you have also done yourself a disservice. Your career will be full of starts and stops. The ones who stay the long haul are the ones that are the winners in the long run. Look at the successful CEO's and business leaders around the world–most have been with the organisation over 10 years and the organisation awards them for their commitment to organisation before self. An employee who does not see the benefits of the organisation before one's can never be a business leader or CEO.

The second aspect is **compensation.** Many join a firm and at the end of the first year, start negotiating for a 50% hike. If somebody believes their value is up by 50% in one year, have got to also believe that it is the firm that provided opportunity for significant value increase. So, isn't it fair to share the spoils and treat the career and compensation opportunity not like a 20–20 cricket match? Or treat yourself as if you are a stock? In that case, you should be also ready for downward movement–but no employee is ever willing to take a salary cut.

The third aspect is the **utilisation of company resources**. The padding of expense reports is the oldest trick in the book. People get paid well enough nowadays not to have to try to use these tricks. An employer definitely notices what is going on, but may not confront you. However the employer does end up making a judgment call. If a person cannot be trusted on an expense report, how can the person be trusted with all the company's finances? For short term benefits, don't lose out on the significant long term gains that can come your way.

Employee ethics–the basics

- Honour commitments
- Don't be greedy
- Don't abuse corporate resources.
- Be ethical

And lastly, I want to remind everybody that the world is a very small place, and what goes around, comes around. I cannot tell you how many times I run into people who I met 20 years ago, and when I meet them, they are in a position to make a judgment call that can affect me personally and professionally. Remember this when you try to shortchange your current employer. Don't burn your bridges, it will come back to haunt you sooner that you think.

Chapter 27

Setting up Your Firm's Oscars

He has won the company Oscar third time in a row and look, even the trophy is smiling!

There are various ways to motivate individuals in an organisation to perform efficiently. Cash motivation in terms of incentives and bonus does work. However, in most cases it is only the individual who knows how he/she has performed. For most employees, organisation wide recognition motivates them to drive their performance and plays an important role for achieving individual and team goals. There are different ways in which this can be done. One of the most effective ways we have seen is institutionalising awards. And it is better if it comes from the Chairman's Office. These awards can be in individual and team categories, and usually announced annually. The responsibility to operationalise the awards usually lies with the HR department.

To begin with, finalise the award categories, which should be **no more than 4–6**, or it may lose its charm. In individual categories, it could be 'Best Employee', 'Best Salesman' or 'Best Manager'. In team categories, it could 'Best Business Unit', 'Best Support Department', or 'Best Project Team'. The last one is important if there are strategic projects being implemented, with multi-department staff working on it. Next is to develop the **measurement criteria**, which need to be simple, objective, and easy to understand by all staff, so when the awards are administered, everyone understands why a particular team or individual is the winner. The measurement criteria are usually a mix of data available in the system (revenue, profit, cost reduction) and qualitative inputs (contribution as team member, feedback from supervisors/peers). It is important that the qualitative factors are also quantified, so a final score can be calculated, to decide on the winners. Next, develop the detailed terms of reference for the awards outlining how the awards will be administered. These will include the timeframe to be considered for the award, criteria for nominations of each award, criteria for short-listing individuals/teams, method for evaluation and calculation of points. The necessary forms need to be finalised at this stage, which can be used for nominations and evaluation.

To ensure that the awards evaluation is unbiased, **appoint a panel**, which would act as the jury. The panel usually consists of senior management executives, from cross functional departments. The panel receives nominations, scans them and identifies the short-listed teams/individuals, conducts necessary checks/interviews, finalises scores for short-listed participants and selects the winning individuals/teams. At the end, what kind of awards will be handed out, need to be finalised. These could be a mix of cash, trophy, certificate, and maybe a family holiday or other gifts.

Your Oscars framework

- 4–6 Awards
- Select measurement criteria
- Appoint a panel
- Communicate companywide
- Recognise winners publicly

An important step now is to announce and **communicate** the awards scheme introduction across the organisation. A bit of hype helps at this stage. This is usually done through special announcements from the HR department. To create excitement, various media should be used through teaser campaigns prior to the launch, announcements through special newsletters, e-mails, intranet, and posters. Details of the award schemes and its administration can be published as a booklet and uploaded on the intranet. Since employees will have queries, contact details of the concerned people need to be communicated, so people can contact them for clarifications.

The annual **awards ceremony** needs to be organised as a special function, attended by all employees, and the winners felicitated by the Chairman, recognising the winners' contributions. Public recognition will drive the employees to enhance their contribution, as individuals and as a team.

Chapter 28

Effective Sales Force Compensation

After selling the entire inventory, the sales staff has given us an ultimatum—they'll start collections only after the committee finalises the salesforce compensation programme!

Many organisations around the world have back-offices that are many times larger than the front office. In the quest of HR departments finding a balance for compensation for all employees, they sometimes forget the need to truly incentivise the people who generate the revenue.

At a strategic level, many have been debated **whether sales incentives need to be capped**. The answer lies in separating sales jobs into two distinct categories. First is 'Seller/Business' model which typically includes life insurance, stock brokers, real estate, mortgage brokers to name a few. In this category, company's business is purely selling and commoditised. Here sales is individual dependent and carries risk of the salespeople taking customers along with them if they leave. This necessitates sales incentives be paid as a proportion of profits/revenues without any cap. Second is 'Seller/Representative' model and in this case, salespeople act as an employee-representative of the company and its products. Here the company manages payouts within a prescribed target pay range and management uses market data to establish these amounts. Through careful incentive design and assignment of accurate quotas, the sales incentive plan successfully can manage payouts within a preferred range and is capped with market benchmarks.

Pay-Mix is ratio of 'Base Salary-to-Incentive at Risk' and expressed as a % of target pay. An aggressive sales incentive strategy favors a **lower base salary with a higher at-risk** incentive because these plans ensure variable costs, drive volume performance and are more motivational in nature. Degree of persuasion in a sales job defines nature of Pay-Mix. For example, if sales rely on persuasion skills of the seller (door-to-door sales) then base salary will be low and at-risk portion will be significant. However, if the company's product/services provide rationale for customer purchase (brand equity), then persuasion role of salesperson is less relevant and base salary is higher, while at-risk proportion is smaller.

An effective sales compensation strategy synchronises **three critical processes**—Forecasting, Quota Allocation and Sales Compensation. Forecasting develops an overall goal number for a fiscal year and Sales need to participate to ensure realistic numbers. Quota allocation breaks down forecast into individual goals for each salesperson. It is preferred that there is no over-assignment of quotas that exceed forecast, nor 'breakage' that leaves some fraction of forecast number unassigned to sales resources.

Many reasons exist for a weak sales compensation strategy including questionable quotas, poor formula mechanics and broken administrative systems. Often overlooked by sales compensation specialists is 'Design' of the sales job. Sales organisations need to realign jobs with emerging/changing market conditions. Without effective buyer segmentation tools, sales organisations allow sales jobs to become 'blended' and 'corrupted'. Typically, tendency is to attempt to resolve these job design errors with sales incentive 'patches', resulting in too many measures and rewarding too many non-productive activities.

Sales compensation strategy creates a sales management solution. Critically, the Sales department 'owns' responsibility for design and administration of the sales plan, but others must contribute to design effort. Using a task force approach, HR can ensure target pay levels are consistent with market, Marketing can ensure proper focus on products and Finance can provide revenue, cost and profit objectives.

Sales compensation strategy is **a mission-critical pay program**. And, is a high-stake, high-visibility pay system that requires focus and comprehensive design support.

Chapter 29

Managing Employee Exits

Now, go ahead and tell me all to make this organisation the best place to work—after you leave!

With a large number of opportunities, some employees are treating companies like revolving doors. In the past, the argument was that some employees (generally Middle East) were on 2–3 year contracts, one can't expect loyalty. Today, many employees don't even complete their contract period. Many don't understand the damage they are doing to their résumés by changes every year. At some point, it will catch up with them. This chapter focuses on the organisation's challenge.

Firstly, include clauses in the employment contract that **dissuade short term behavior**–both carrots and sticks. Carrots include sign-on bonuses that need to be refunded if the person leaves before a certain period of time (e.g. one year), guaranteed part of year 1/2 bonus, international training commitments, etc. Sticks include that all costs including internal/external training cost need to be reimbursed, holding part of the annual bonus back that will be paid with interest only three years from start, and strong non-competes.

Still resignations will come in. If the employee has worked for two and a half to three years, and has done a good job, and the **exit is being handled by the employee professionally** (e.g. honoring the notice period) the conversation needs to be cordial, and an attempt should be made to understand why the employee is leaving and to retain the employee. These conversations cannot be initiated by the employee's boss, but two levels up and HR. In an attempt to retain, at no time should the employee be given a sense of his/her being indispensable (nobody is), no significant company rules should be altered, and the conversation should give a sense that it is in the interest of both that the decision should be reviewed.

If the employee is resigning after a short period of time, and the **conduct is not appropriate**—for instance, she/he is not willing to give notice period or is on unplanned leave—one needs to be firm. Any violation of contract terms must be taken seriously and acted upon, and whatever penalties are applicable, need to be applied. If one does not take a strong position in these matters, word quickly spreads that management is not serious about contract terms. There are two views on whether a person should be allowed to serve notice period or exited immediately. I think it depends on whether there is somebody to take over the assignment immediately or that may take some time.

Many organisations conduct **exit interviews**. While I think in general it is a good idea, its value is limited. Most employees don't really provide honest answers to the questions. Communicating exits need to be done carefully through an organisation. If the conduct of the person exiting was unacceptable, this should be explained to employees. Those that are leaving and have done a good job and leaving gracefully, should be congratulated, and wished well. They are future ambassadors of the company.

Always advise employees to leave on good terms. Unfortunately, for them, the world is very small, and they are likely to run into you again, sooner rather than later.

I am concluding with a couple of closing points. Firstly, one will panic less in exit situations when a succession plan is in place, and one can quickly identify another resource from within the organisation. And secondly, never get personal or emotional about it. At the end of the day, it's just a job!

Conclusion

Well, hopefully you have enjoyed the book.

More importantly, I hope you will find use for some of the suggestions I have made in dealing with the HR challenges that you are faced with, everyday. If it is any solace, you know that managing the relationship with your wife itself is a challenge. Imagine having to do that with hundreds of people. It's not a challenge for the faint hearted and some of the world's best CEOs still haven't figured it out.

The solution is to use your best judgment, use the best external and internal advise you can get, be strong, put your hand on your heart, and do the right thing.

After all they are all human beings with families and without them, your company will have no soul.

Author's Profile

Sanjiv is the Managing Director of Cedar Management Consulting International, a global management consulting firm with over 800 clients and a network of 16 offices worldwide. Cedar has won the BME Award for Best Advisory Firm for 2010 and 2011.

For over 25 years, he has worked with CEOs and Boards across the world in the development of their strategies and the transformation of their businesses, in many industry sectors. He is a thought leader in the Balanced Scorecard, the world's leading Strategy Deployment and Enterprise Performance Management framework. Clients include AT&T, Whirlpool, RadioShack, Sara Lee, Abu Dhabi Commercial Bank, Airtel, Hero Group, Singapore Stock Exchange, Mitsubishi amongst many others.

Sanjiv has an MBA from the NYU Stern School of Business, and has completed the Advanced Management Program from Harvard Business School. He also completed his engineering from MNIT, Jaipur. Sanjiv writes regularly for Business India, Banker Middle East, and Gulf News. He has been a Chapter Chair for the Young Presidents Organisation, on the Alumni Council of NYU Stern, and recently appointed to the Board of a Trident Group Company.

Sanjiv has two sons, Sahil and Jai, both study at NYU. His wife Monica has been a teacher at Sophia College for many years. He enjoys travelling the world, playing the guitar, and is hoping to be a good golfer!

You can reach him at: Sanjiv.Anand@cedar-consulting.com